DEALING *with*
DEMONS

3 - 3 - 21

DESTINY IMAGE BOOKS BY BOB LARSON

Jezebel

Curse Breaking

Demon Proofing Prayers

DEALING *with* DEMONS

An Introductory Guide to
EXORCISM *&* DISCERNING
EVIL SPIRITS

BOB LARSON

DESTINY IMAGE® PUBLISHERS, INC.

P.O. Box 310, Shippensburg, PA 17257-0310

"Promoting Inspired Lives."

This book and all other Destiny Image and Destiny Image Fiction books are available at Christian bookstores and distributors worldwide.

Cover design by Eileen Rockwell

For more information on foreign distributors, call 717-532-3040.

Reach us on the Internet: www.destinyimage.com.

ISBN 13 TP: 978-0-7684-0967-3

ISBN 13 eBook: 978-0-7684-0968-0

For Worldwide Distribution, Printed in the U.S.A.

3 4 5 6 7 8 / 20 19 18 17 16

DEDICATION

To the brave men and women whose stories are told on these pages, I dedicate this book. In spite of their bondage and suffering, they courageously reached out for help. Through tears and brokenness, they revealed the deepest secrets of their souls, often telling me what they'd never told anyone before. They laid aside their shame, anger, and fear to expose the terrors of evil of which few speak. Through much prayer and intensive probing, they allowed the Holy Spirit to uncover the schemes of Satan so they could be liberated. Today, they are living testaments to the hope of a changed life, through the power and presence of Jesus Christ.

And, of course, I also dedicate this book to my wonderful wife and three precious daughters. They shared my time and life with those who had nowhere else to turn, and for whom our ministry held the key to their true freedom. Thanks to my family for understanding the unique, and often misunderstood, commitment and anointing of this ministry to heal the brokenhearted and set the captives free!

CONTENTS

Introduction and Reader's Guide. 9

Chapter One   Cracking Satan's Code. 17

Chapter Two   From the Hollers to Hell. 31

Chapter Three   The Fingerprint of the Family 53

Chapter Four   The God Factor. 67

Chapter Five   Witchcraft and the Occult 83

Chapter Six   Sleuthing Spirits of Body and Soul 99

Chapter Seven Second That Emotion 127

Chapter Eight Closing the Demon Door of Trauma. 163

INTRODUCTION
AND READER'S GUIDE

JESUS TALKED. HE TALKED A LOT. FOR EXAMPLE, HIS SERMON ON the Mount takes up three whole chapters of the Gospel of Matthew, chapters five, six, and seven. And remember, what we have in Scripture is not a verbatim account. It's like reading a Reuters or Associated Press report with the main points, the most important quotes, and the central ideas condensed and emphasized. What's recorded in the Bible's account of the Sermon on the Mount may take ten minutes to read, even at a good rate of intellectual absorption. In reality, it lasted an entire day. Likewise, the lengthy Sermon on the Plain in Luke chapter six is another marathon message.

But Christ also talked a lot on an individual basis. Consider the so-called "woman at the well" account of chapter four of John. Like the Sermon on the Mount, there's no indication of actual length. We can surmise that it might have lasted at least an hour or even several hours, as Christ lovingly drew out the life-facts of this Samaritan woman. Later in the book we'll consider the demon-possession account of the Syrophoenician woman whose faith Christ sorely tested in Mark chapter seven. His interchanges with her went on for some time, as He challenged the depth of her faith.

My point? When Jesus ministered to people He took time. He touched their feelings and illustrated to us how to elicit the deepest needs of people, which are often hidden behind wounded emotions. In some ways, Christ was the first psychotherapist, using a process of listening and talking to bring hope and healing to emotional disorders. Certainly, Christ ultimately intervened supernaturally and miraculously. But preceding that, it's obvious that He met people right where they were psychologically, even when they were in the midst of intense pain.

Consider, for a moment, these interchanges with people to whom Christ ministered. They are instances in which Jesus cast out demons.

- "What is your name?" (Mark 5:9, a question directed toward the demon Legion.)

- "How long has this been happening to him?" (Mark 9:21, a question asked of the man with a demon possessed son who tried to kill himself.)

- "It is not good to take the children's bread and throw it to the little dogs." (Matthew 15:26, though stated affirmatively, is actually a rhetorical device used to provoke the woman whose daughter was demon-possessed.)

In each case, Jesus knew the answer. After all, He was fully God incarnate. Why then, did He ask questions to which He already knew the answer? He did it in order to demonstrate that deliverance isn't always an act of power-packed intervention and that more often it is a painstakingly slow process of well-asked questions and much-analyzed answers. Like good Christian counseling, the path to an exorcism is paved with listening skills and Spirit-led inquiries. It is in this give-and-take that the keys to winning in spiritual warfare are often unveiled.

That is why in this book the reader will learn the value of a deliberate, intricate approach to setting people free from all forms of demonic bondage. Frankly, the portion of the Christianized world that *does* believe in exorcism and deliverance must discard some old ways of attempting to expel evil from the lives of individuals. Those deliverance ministers and counselors who have tried these insufficient approaches must honestly admit that they really haven't worked very well. Either people didn't get fully free, or their freedom didn't stick. Delivered individuals were all too soon back to their old ways, and sometimes much worse than before.

Allow me to ask some pointed, uncomfortable questions that challenge the traditional way all too many deliverance ministers have approached the demonic.

Why would you bombard a demonic manifestation with lengthy high-volume tirades against evil, when what's really needed is to methodically get the relevant information that will destroy the power base of the demons, which usually involves sins, unbroken curses, and ungodly soul ties?

Why would you rely primarily on unprovable "prophetic" revelations and highly subjective "words from the Lord" to guide the deliverance process, when an effective interrogation of the demons can get to the root of the matter faster and more objectively?

Why would you think it is more spiritual to keep demons from speaking or "acting up," when Christ clearly allowed demons to verbalize and also permitted demonic manifestations in His presence, even in the synagogue/church?

The time is long overdue for those who say they believe in deliverance to reassess their motives and methods. The deliverance ministry has been rejected or ostracized in most mainstream evangelical churches. Part of the abstention is due to cessationist theology, the idea that the miracle of casting out demons ended with the passing of the apostolic age. But there is another reason many conscientious Christian leaders eschew the idea of casting out demons, even among those who have a continuationist approach to spiritual gifts and the miraculous. To some Christian leaders, a lot of deliverance ministry is just plain weird and does more harm than good. Why should they allow exorcism a place in the body-life of a congregation?

My answer to those accusations may surprise the reader. In many cases, I agree. Deliverance has often been performed with few sound psychological approaches and far too many outlying behavioral practices that reasonable people can see have the potential to be emotionally injurious. There has sometimes been a lack of proper ethical boundaries and much unwise dependence on supposed supernatural revelations. Critics seldom witness the hard work of spiritually investigative approaches to battling Satan.

Some of the ways that certain ministers do deliverance is embarrassingly inept and potentially damaging to mentally unsound people. Often, good common sense and empathetic concern for the one seeking help take a back seat to an authoritarian approach that borders on the abusive. I pray that what's in this book will display enough depth and caution to counter-balance all the bad "press" given to the ministry of casting out demons. We must stop giving deliverance a bad name. My desire is to show that a proper approach to it can be an adjunct to the help provided by the therapeutic community; deliverance can assist those in social services as well as those in psychiatry and psychology.

GUIDELINES FOR READING THIS BOOK

There are several approaches in my writing style that need explaining.

1. I sometimes refer to the possessed individual as the "host," a fairly common term in secular literature about the subject.

2. At times I also use the word "client" as a way of designating the person who seeks help from a deliverance minister.

3. In my frame of reference, the term "deliverance" refers collectively to all that is involved in the process of setting a person free from demonic bondage; thus, deliverance includes inner healing work and various prayers of curse-breaking as well as approaches to forgiveness and reconciliation. "Exorcism" is the act of actually expelling an evil spirit, the final step in the deliverance process.

4. A deliverance minister is any concerned Christian, usually a lay person, who feels called

to engage in the spiritual calling of exposing and casting out demons.

5.   The true identities of the individuals referred to in cited case studies have been changed. None of the real names are the same as those used in the telling of these stories.

6.   On occasion the facts of more than one case have been combined, when the essence of the deliverance process is not compromised by this literary device. This approach allows for greater brevity in writing, without having to change the context of a story and reestablish its circumstances a second time.

7.   Several theological assumptions are foundational in the accounts of possession and exorcism. First, Christians can be demonized. Secondly, all believers in Jesus have been conferred authority to cast out demons.

8.   Deliverance and exorcism are normative to Christian belief and living. Our International School of Exorcism® has several courses devoted to an intense study of church history. The courses reveal how integral to early church life the casting out of demons was.

9.   The ministries of deliverance and exorcism are a mandate from Christ, not an optional aspect of Christian teaching and evangelism. We take seriously the fact that the Great Commission

of Mark 16:15–17 declares that the first sign of the gospel's integrity and authenticity is the demonstration of Christ's command, "In My name they will cast out demons."

10.   My intended audience is comprised of interested lay people and the clergy, but also those involved in counseling ministries. As these professionals encounter cases of demonic possession, we want to help them understand that there are acceptable approaches to emotional healing and behavioral integration that are psychologically sound.

I now invite the reader to join me in discovering a whole new way of looking at a much maligned ministry. The ancient spiritual art of exorcism is much needed in our troubled times, and it is alive and well in many ministries.

Chapter One

CRACKING SATAN'S CODE

WILLIAM WASN'T EXACTLY A SLOUCH. HE HAD EARNED TWO PhDs, one from Harvard. He arranged to speak with me via Skype in what we call a Personal Spiritual Encounter session. At the time of our meeting he was in France doing research for a major corporation. Not exactly the kind of person you'd expect to be suffering from an early midlife crisis. But he was, and his condition was desperate.

In fact, William was depressed to the point of considering suicide. With his career in full swing, he was contemplating an early exit from life. Oh, and William professed to be an evangelical Christian, one of those rare intellectuals who claim to be "born again." He had a loving and supportive wife and grown children who were success-ful in their own right. What could possibly have driven him to the point of such despair?

The standard psychological, therapeutic model likely would have included medication to deal with his sense of hopelessness. Nothing's necessarily wrong with that. Cognitive behavioral therapy might have suggested that William take a more rational approach to the facts of his evident success and focus on the good he'd accomplished. That too could have helped. But already William had tried everything, and still he was no better. At that point, who're you gonna call? An exorcist?

In this case, yes. In William's words, "I figured that someone who knows as much as you do about demons, who deals with the extreme edges of evil, might have insights that standard psychological intervention and typical pastoral counseling would not consider."

But I didn't do what William expected; I didn't whip out my cross and holy anointing oil. I first talked about his life as any good counselor would. But my focus was more specific. I wanted to know the dynamics of the family in which he was raised. I reasoned that if the devil had anything to do with William's melancholy it must be rooted somewhere in the messages he got while growing up. That's not Freudian; that's plain wisdom.

THROW MOMMA FROM THE TRAIN?

It didn't take much conversation for me to discover that William's mother was a key factor. She had inherited a lucrative family business and her husband, William's biological father, went along for the ride. William's dad was, as we say, an Ahab kind of guy. Not too individualistic or self-motivated. He'd found a cushy life with a rich wife and wasn't going to rock that boat. Mom made all the important decisions and controlled the money. As long as there was plenty of that, why should Ahab-dad bother?

William described his mother in bitter tones. She was controlling, manipulative, and domineering. (If you want more details on this kind of person, check out my book *Jezebel: Defeating Your #1 Spiritual Enemy*.) He could never please her. No achievement was good enough. No accolade led to an "atta-boy." Mom was cold, emotionally sterile, and commanding to the point of mapping out William's entire career path. Here he was in his late 40s, doing exactly what mother wanted—and hating every moment.

After about 30 minutes' interaction we hit upon a defining moment in William's life. When he was eight and had shown some interest in music and the arts, he had skipped across the room singing a tune he'd learned on TV. His mother sternly stopped him. "Don't you have more important things to do?" she scolded. "Enough of that foolishness. There's no future in filling your head with tunes. Get back to your room and study. You're going to be a great businessman someday, just like your grandfather."

William never hummed a song again, at least not when Mom was around. But his musical moratorium couldn't quiet the raging sense of anger inside. He grew to hate his mother—and he grew to hate his mother's God. That's the other factor.

Mom was religious to a fault. Everything was done in good order and with pious rectitude. William's baptism was a society footnote. His confirmation was attended by all the extended family. She did frown on the zeal he expressed when, as a teen, he started hanging out with more charismatic types of Christians. But as long as he was religious, she was happy. For

William, however, even though he prayed to receive Christ as his personal Savior at a small Pentecostal church he'd visited, God was never as close as he desired. And there was no way of finding the Lord's will for his life. Everything in his future had been carefully laid out in the matrix provided by Mother.

As William spilled out to me all these heart-wrenching details of his early life I could see him getting more and more agitated. He began swearing. His anger escalated. Profane, vile words spewed forth. According to William, he'd never had this conversation with anyone. It had never been safe for him to tell another person how much he despised his mother.

Gradually, William's personal emotional venting morphed into a more demonic sort of vileness. On my computer screen, I could see the behavioral changes that alerted me to a more demonic element in his words and expressions.

Moments later I was confronting an evil spirit of Hate. The demon claimed a right to William; the spiritual opening had come from his severe anger toward his mother. The demon laughed heartily, so proud of how he had used Mom to warp the normal love of a child for his mother and turn it into something diabolical.

I walked William through several stages of healing ministry: emotional ownership of his bitterness, forgiveness toward his mother, the breaking of curses of generational control, and then the expulsion of the demons which had so cleverly turned a biological heritage of potential greatness into self-loathing and self-destruction.

There is much more to William's story, and I will not cover it completely here. My purpose in the telling about him is to introduce you, the reader, to the concept that dealing with demons involves more than formalistic prayers or shouting vociferously at supposed evil entities.

Confronting demonic forces should involve a willingness to more deeply understand human behavior and uncover the clever ways that the devil wends his way into our lives. I call this process "cracking Satan's code." It's much like the way a cryptologist pores over minute details to decipher the underlying message that is hidden to most observers. In the process there is an ultimate question to be answered: Are the problems of the individual in question the result of life in a fallen world, or is the devil at work in devious and seemingly undetectable ways?

THE DEVIL MADE HIM DO IT

Most of my readers are too young to remember the African-American comedian Flip Wilson, famous in the '70s for his in-drag Geraldine character. With high heels and bouffant hair, Wilson as Geraldine would obliquely recount some scandalous behavior, arch an eyebrow and retort, "The devil made me do it." Audiences howled with laughter because everyone knew that blaming the devil was Geraldine's excuse for every unsavory behavior.

That lame self-pardon has since become the disparaging tagline used by those opposed to people like me who minister inner healing, deliverance, and exorcism. We're often accused of shifting the responsibility to Satan for any number of ills. Even Christian critics are quick to dismiss the idea of demonic interference in human affairs, preferring to cite the inability to overcome the flesh as the real culprit for human failing. Psychologists have any number of labels to pin on behavior which is unacceptable, even pathological.

But our collective social consciousness is regularly shaken by events so evil they defy humanistic efforts to wish away the idea of absolute evil. A deranged killer opens fire on movie patrons in an Aurora, Colorado, theater. A social misfit acts out of racial hatred and kills nine people praying in a Charleston, South Carolina, church. A pressure-cooker bomb explodes in Boston at a sporting event frequented by families.

As a society, we listen to the opinions of cable news pundits who fan the flames of fear and give few answers. We observe court psychiatrists on both sides of the insanity defense divide. We're told that some psychotic episode detached the killer from reality, or that a narcissistic, self-focused outlook prevented the murderer from understanding the consequences of his actions. But inside we know that something so bad must have its roots in a dimension outside the realm of ordinary human existence. Something diabolical, something supernatural, something too debased for rational minds to grasp must have influenced, even overpowered, the thinking of individuals we classify as deranged mass murderers.

Even when preachers follow up such hideous happenings with comments like, "This was demonic," or "Satan did this," they often don't really mean what they say. Modern theology and evangelical thinking have distanced themselves from the idea that the devil and demons play any kind of significant role in human behavior. Part of the problem is that, if they took Satan seriously, what would they really do about it? By and large they've expunged the idea of casting out demons with any kind of frequency. Exorcism just isn't an option. What's left but to minimize the role of evil spirits and relegate their intervention in human affairs to infrequent at best?

Three decades ago I became involved in the case of the infamous serial killer Henry Lee Lucas, at his request. I traveled to the small Texas town where he was first jailed. At that time, accused of just one crime, he began to spin tales of a kill-count so horrible it defied imagination. (He was eventually executed for one killing, and his claim of hundreds of victims is still disputed.) For hours I sat in his jail cell (which you could do in Texas thirty years ago), as he described to me in detail his killing sprees. The accounts were cruel beyond imagination. For example, he told me that he often kept some body part of a victim with him as an offering to Satan. The devil had told him that as long as he did this, he would never be caught. He described once being stopped by a highway patrolman while he had the human head of a victim next to him on the passenger's seat, covered by a coat. True to the devil's pledge, the officer never investigated him further.

Before his execution, Lucas told me that the devil made him do it, or something approximating that contention. So did teen killer Sean Sellers, another murderer in whose case I became involved. Sean told me many times how he performed rituals to worship the devil, particularly the night he conjured demons and subsequently murdered his mother and stepfather in cold blood. Before his execution Sellers also claimed that he was driven by demons to kill and had no recollection of actually pulling the trigger.

This book isn't about mass murderers or unfathomable killing sprees. But these incidents serve to underpin the idea that certain kinds of human conduct, including bloodthirsty crimes, are the result of demonic influence. You may never cross the path of a mass murderer, but you do have acquaintances, friends, and loved ones whose precipitous actions defy reasonable understanding.

They act out of context in ways that are inconsistent with their normative behavior.

The husband who suddenly stops going to church and spends his evenings at the bars. The wife who confesses to an affair when everything in the marriage seemed to be going well. The child whose actions turn bizarre and rebellious after having been raised in the church and walking closely to the Lord. Friends or extended family members who are caught stealing, using illegal drugs, frequenting strip joints, drinking heavily—all actions completely contrary to the way they previously comported themselves. And it seems to come on somewhat quickly, as if an internal moral switch had been flipped and those things this person had held dear suddenly hold no more meaning.

Certainly there are many reasons for abrupt changes in behavior and moral conduct. There's no point in evaluating all of those factors here. What I'm going to focus on is the possibility that aberrational actions may be precipitated or strongly influenced by evil spirits, that the devil really did make them do it, not in the sense that Satan made human puppets of them, but rather that the compulsion of demonic forces was too strong to resist. Most important, I want the reader to understand that such illogical and destructive behavior is predictable—and preventable.

Unthinkable behaviors are correctable, if you have the right diagnosis. I audaciously claim, after decades of ministering exorcism and deliverance to tens of thousands of people, that spiritual forensics are possible. Yes, you can actually spot the fingerprint of Satan, and you can determine if any action or behavior is essentially demonically motivated. You can crack the code to Satan's schemes and reveal the clandestine evil machinations that are at work.

Wouldn't it be a wonderful thing if you personally could crack that code with friends and loved ones? Wouldn't it bring comfort to understand what's behind their inconsistent actions and to know how to pray for them and minister to them? Being able to identify the fingerprint of Satan would revolutionize Christian counseling and inner healing ministries. And it would radically change the lives of those you love and care about.

I'VE GOT A SECRET

I am about to reveal to you secrets that it's taken me a lifetime to discover. I will share with you on these pages what has taken me decades to synthesize. But let me first tell you what you *will not* find in this book. This book is *not*:

- A rehashing of anything I've written in any of my other books.

- A restatement of what's available on my DVDs or published blogs.

- Material exclusive to the training in our online International School of Exorcism.

A further word about that. Our online International School of Exorcism represents the highest level of knowledge and training that this ministry has to offer. What's in this book is not duplicated there. My prayer is that once you've read the book you'll see how indispensable it is to go on to enroll in the School. It's in the School's courses of instruction that you'll learn the biblical and historical foundation for deliverance. You'll be trained in the knowledge of how Satan's kingdom operates and how to dismantle the devil's curses, legal rights, and spiritual strongholds.

You'll be equipped to actually minister inner healing and cast out demons in the name of Jesus.

The School of Exorcism has the tools you'll need to take your anointing and calling from the Lord to the next level and to become actively engaged in spiritual warfare, confronting the forces of darkness. I pray that after you read this book, you'll want to do that.[1]

But for now, your interest may be simply to understand what is negatively affecting those you love and whether their problems stem all or in part from the work of demons. Plus, you may want practical advice on how to get started helping those you're concerned about. You want to know if, like me, you can spot the fingerprint of Satan and determine that a certain situation is largely the result of demons. Is that person oppressed by the devil? You want to crack the code!

Having this information will change your whole approach to spiritual intervention in people's lives. If someone's problems are emotional, you can seek the help of the medical and psychological community so they can address the matter with medication and/or therapy. If the individual merely needs a deeper biblical basis for faith and behavior, then the answer may be as simple as finding a good Bible-teaching church with an active fellowship and support groups.

But if demons are involved, will you know what to do? And how do you even figure out in the first place that the fingerprint of Satan is on someone's life? I have been determining this on a daily basis and will show you how to make similar evaluations.

Some years ago our ministry launched a program called Personal Spiritual Encounters, one-on-one sessions of an hour or more that quickly identify where the devil and demons are at work in someone's life. We conduct many such sessions every week at our ministry offices in Phoenix, Arizona, or in one of the cities where I hold weekly seminars. Because over time I have developed the spiritual acuity to operate with the gift of discerning evil spirits I can often meet with a complete stranger and within a few minutes determine whether that person's problems are primarily emotional, situational, behavioral, mental, or demonic—or some combination of these. By God's grace, I spot the fingerprint of Satan quickly and effectively, and I can quickly crack the code.

I don't expect that, by just reading this book, you will be able to immediately duplicate my particular anointing and years of experience. But what if you could replicate even a small portion of what I do? If I can teach you in this book a portion of the spiritual skills I've developed, how much further ahead would you be to solving so many challenges in your own life, as well as helping those around you out of their dire circumstances? And if you were to go on and enroll in our School of Exorcism (www .internationalschoolofexorcism.org), how much more might the Lord use you to bring healing to many brokenhearted people?

As you know, in forensic science, fingerprints (along with DNA) are all-important. Often, the fingerprints left at the crime scene lead to the conviction of the killer. With the fingerprint you can trace who did it, and then begin to uncover why the crime took place. That's what you'll learn in this book—where and how to find Satan's fingerprints on a spiritual "crime." Whether it's you or someone else, consider what you can uncover about the individual's actions in question.

Was there a generational curse that was embedded in the spiritual DNA and sprang to life for some identifiable reason?

What influence did one's experiences as a child have on objectionable behavior that happens decades later?

Was there a soul-bond that passed on evil from another living individual, a kind of soul transference from one to the other?

How did past church participation and theological influences alter how life and relationships would be perceived?

What parent-child factors caused problems to arise later in life that seem disconnected from conscious thinking?

Are health issues linked to mental problems of depression, anxiety, fearfulness, and worthlessness? And how are these issues exploited by demons?

Which life traumas are the most significant to evaluate as factors which may have opened doors to demons?

How should diagnosed mental health issues be treated—as the causes or the products of severe demonic attack?

Which sicknesses and infirmities should be considered the work of evil spirits and how can that be determined?

PERSPECTIVE

By now, I'm sure you understand our quest in this book. Not to be flippant about Flip, but *did* the devil do it? Just knowing the answer to that question produces a sea change in how people and their problems should be approached. Even though integrating spiritual wholeness of body and soul with an understanding of spiritual deliverance is a much-neglected discipline in most Christian circles, you can change that dynamic with what you'll learn on the pages that follow. Once you know how to spot the fingerprint of Satan, you'll be on your way to changing your own life and making a radical impact on the lives of those you love.

With this information in hand, you *will* learn to crack the code.

NOTE

1. To enroll in the International School of Exorcism, simply go to www.internationalschoolofexorcism.org.

Chapter Two

FROM THE HOLLERS TO HELL

FANS OF THE '50S CRIME SERIES *DRAGNET* REMEMBER WELL THE oft-quoted line of detective Joe Friday, "Just the facts, ma'am, just the facts."

Friday's droll response to some running-off-at-the-mouth character symbolized his no-nonsense approach to solving mysteries. In each episode there was always some person who was being interviewed about the crime in question. That individual would go off on a tangent giving far more information than was needed, embellishing the most simple of events with verbal flourishes of irrelevancy. It was then that Friday (actor Jack Webb) would look somewhat disgustedly at his partner, "Frank Smith," then back at the interviewee and say, "Just the facts, ma'am."

JUST THE FACTS, MA'AM!

It's the Joe Friday approach to dealing with demons that's crucial to success in spiritual warfare. Often it's the most basic facts about an individual's personal history that give clues to demonic intrusion into their lives. Consider the crucial role that elementary information plays in determining what the devil has done and knowing how to crack the code to Satan's machinations. Just the facts. For example, it's important to know:

- Age

- Residency location

- Occupation

- Education

- Marital status

- Extended family

- Ethnicity

- Cultural identity

- Religious history

- Current religious affiliation

On the surface this list seems very basic and not too insightful. But there is more to be learned than the reader might suppose. These ten things alone could be sufficient to reasonably determine the extent to which Satan is operating in one's life. Those who have attended my seminars or watched our YouTube Exorcism Channel know that some form of these ten bits of information introduce almost every exorcism in which I engage. Knowing these basics gives a thumbnail sketch, a snapshot of who the person is and what constitutes his or her self-perception and place in the world. Agreed, these designations are broad brushstrokes of analysis, by nature categorical. Even so, such generalizations have often proven to be good indicators as to how to proceed with ministry. They provide a good place to start, and the case of Edna is an excellent example.

EVIL IN APPALACHIA

Seated on the front row at one of my seminars, Edna seemed the most unlikely person in the room in need of deliverance. With greying hair, inauspicious appearance, and a slight smile, she looked stereotypically like the grandmother that she was. Indeed, a great-grandmother. Yet when I approached her for prayer there was no mistaking the incongruous, low growl that came from her throat. As I stretched forth a hand to anoint her with holy oil, her head jerked sideways to avert my touch. When I gently placed a Bible on her head, the response was immediate and violent. She thrashed about convulsively, and it took several strong men to hold her still.

As her eyes blinked in self-awareness and her own mind returned to consciousness, she was completely oblivious to what had just happened. Such a precipitous manifestation indicated some kind of strong demonic presence. So, using the ten-point template above, I began quizzing her about the basics of her personal history.

Edna was raised in the "hollers" of West Virginia, in impoverished Appalachia. Though in her early 70s now, her personal trauma dated back to when she was 14 years of age. Raped by a man more than twice her age, she was forced into a "shotgun" wedding. Obviously, this wasn't exactly a marriage made in heaven. Of course, true to her Caucasian, 1950s Pentecostal Holiness upbringing, divorce wasn't an option. A lifetime of misery and entrenched anger was. Her disgust and rage toward what she had been subjected to at a barely postpubescent age just got shoved deeper and deeper into her psyche.

There was no religiously acceptable way for Edna to expunge her pain and anger, and no one in her religious circles who wanted to hear her story. No therapy or any kind of counseling was available either. She had never held a job and was (resentfully) financially dependent upon the man she considered a moral monster, her husband. Certainly she still went to church and went through all the right motions of worship and proper spiritual duty. But inside there was a volcano of bitterness waiting to explode. Had she not been a Christian, along the way somewhere murder might have become an option.

Everything I wrote in the previous four paragraphs is information I obtained in a three-minute conversation with her. It contained the facts that I was looking for. Really? In a matter of minutes I had figured out the answers to the above ten criteria and I had a plan of action ready? Yes, and you can, too, if you apply yourself to the proper mental and spiritual disciplines.

Every time I hear of some individual "going postal" and killing at random, whether in a Chattanooga, Tennessee, Army recruiting center or a TV station in Roanoke, Virginia, I say to myself, "If I had just five minutes alone with that person in private, and if the person would be honest in answering my questions, I could tell you exactly why that person did it." More important than figuring out the motive, I could, with the help of Christ, wage spiritual warfare and begin resolving what went wrong.

FINDING THE FINGERPRINT OF SATAN

Fingerprints are marvelous things—those tiny friction ridges on the underside of our fingers. A fingerprint leaves an impression when a digit touches something. In forensic science it has been used for many decades as a serious source of information at a crime scene. Police look on glass, metal objects, or any flat, polished surface for secretions of sweat from the eccrine glands that form patterns on the epidermal edges. When a suspect is arrested, a fingerprint is taken with a special card, usually from the last joint of the thumb or other fingers. Why? The human fingerprint is indelibly defined and remains the same throughout a person's life. And not only criminals are the focus. Lost or dead people can be the subject of a search based on fingerprints. God gave us our epidermal ridges for the purpose of gripping and the sensation of touch; but as a tool of law enforcement or a rescue effort after a natural disaster, a fingerprint may be essential.

Criminals leave fingerprints. Victims of some tragedy may have left fingerprints. And the devil leaves fingerprints, too, telltale patterns that can be identified and deciphered. In the world of crime investigation, this search has become a complex science. Exemplar prints are deliberately collected for inclusion in a data system. Fingerprints may be classified as loops, whorls, or arches. They have plain arches and tented arches, ulnar loops and radial loops. Differences can be assigned to left- and right-hand fingerprints, the particular finger, and the portion of the finger "printed." An algebra-like system of calculation has been devised to further sophisticate this art. Latent, unintended fingerprints are the ones sought by detectives. Picture a CSI crew, soft brushes in hand, poring over a broken piece of glass or a discarded firearm.

For our purposes, here's where it gets interesting. There are several kinds of "fingerprinting" that go beyond the actual impression of a human digit on some surface. Genetic fingerprinting, so much in use by police now, considers DNA patterns. Spectrometric analysis looks at biochemical indicators. Acoustic fingerprints analyze the properties of sound. Digital video can map the face of an individual, revealing one-of-a-kind characteristics. And the list of possibilities goes on and on.

If criminal investigations and health sciences can be so diligent to accurately define individuated identities, why can't we take a similarly objective approach to solving spiritual mysteries? We can, and I'm going to show you how to do it.

Cracking Satan's Code

Evil is not random or capricious. It is deliberate with a defined matrix. More important, these patterns change little. Once you decipher the code of the devil, you know how to spot it under many seemingly different circumstances.

When I start to minister to people they usually begin telling me their problem(s). Often I interrupt to say, "Let me first find out some things about you." Some are offended. They want me to get on with the job of getting out the devil. They want an *exorcism* and they want it *now*. They want deliverance and they want it *yesterday*. Sometimes I call this "drive-through deliverance." But getting the devil out is not the same as keeping him out.

Decipherment, as it's known in the world of code-cracking, typically involves ancient languages or military communications. Today it may also refer to the Human Genome Project, whose goal has been to determine the sequences of base pairs that make up the human DNA. This endeavor has turned out to be the world's largest collaborative biological project. Since it was completed in 2003 about 90 percent of the human genome has been mapped with 99.99 percent accuracy. (By the way, that 90 percent uses only about 10 percent of the available genetic coding material. What's the other 90 percent of the genetic coding material for? Could it include locations in the DNA where generational spiritual and psychological tendencies and patterns are imprinted?) The findings have now been applied to molecular medicine, treatment of cancer, agriculture, anthropology, and animal husbandry, to name a few fields of usage. In all, about 20,000-plus genes have been identified in humans.

Here is a discrepancy I find interesting. Sciences takes such a meticulous approach to the solving of human misery while many involved in deliverance ministries take a shotgun approach, firing ammunition in every direction in hopes of hitting something. Wouldn't it be better to focus more carefully on the DNA indicators ("Deliverance Noteworthy Aspects"—acronym mine) of spiritual warfare? Could it be that Satan's plans are just as complex but just as discoverable? With all the yelling and commanding done in some deliverance circles, often with little permanent results, shouldn't we be considering a more methodical approach?

I've heard the arguments, "Jesus cast out demons quickly," or "He did it with just a word" (see Matthew 8:16). The idea is that ridding someone of demons should be quick and easy. Seldom is that the case. Deliverance can be an arduous process. I genuinely want to make it faster, easier, and more effective. That's why cracking the code is so important. Here, again, are those ten factors to consider when having an initial consultation that may lead to a deliverance session.

Establish a method for deliverance

TEN THINGS TO KNOW TO DEAL WITH DEMONS

Once more, the categories are as follows: (1) age, (2) residency location, (3) occupation, (4) education, (5) marital status, (6) extended family, (7) ethnicity, (8) cultural identity, (9) religious history, and (10) current religious affiliation.

Age

It's helpful to have a general sense of where a person is in the passage from birth to death. The specific age isn't as important as the sense of how the individual has reacted to life's vagaries and vicissitudes. Let's break this down into two basic categories: younger and older, with younger being anywhere from adolescence to the 30s and older approximately age 40 and beyond.

Younger individuals will likely be less serious about life and the consequences of evil. Convincing them to stop a particular behavior in order to be free from Satan may not seem as urgent as it will to someone older. Younger people have a lighter grasp on the spiritual issues of repentance and correction where eternity is concerned. They are also more easily distracted by the things of this world and all its temptations. If evil spirits are embedded in their desire to party, have fun, and indulge in the sexuality and addictions associated with such a lifestyle, they will be harder to dislodge. Younger people are more likely to be drawn to the occult and tend to be more fascinated with the paranormal. That's why they are the demographic target of movies about vampire love and more, such as *Paranormal Activity*.

Most critical is the neurological fact that a younger person may not have the brain development to support cognitive and rational

Younger people may not take deliverance Seriously and may be easily distracted by the world.

38

thinking. Ever wonder why teenagers sometimes do dumb things like jumping off a roof on a skateboard? It's not just chronological development, it's also neurological. The brain just isn't there yet, and the devil knows it. Hence, it can be more challenging to tell such a person what they need to do to be delivered. It can be hard to lead this individual to a place of confession for sin and a willingness to change a behavior that opens the door to evil spirits.

The older individual may also be harder to persuade, but for a different reason: demolishing spiritual strongholds (see 2 Corinthians 10:3–5) gets harder the older the person is. Older people are more set in their ways and perhaps more unwilling to alter the habits which the demons are manipulating. The older one gets, in my counseling experience, the more entrenched the demons are. These evil spirits have been there longer and know all the places of the soul to which they can attach. There are certainly more soul ties with an older person. (This concept is explained in my books *Jezebel* and *Curse Breaking*.) Particularly in the case of an unsaved person or one who is a new Christian, think of all the potential "one-flesh" sexual connections which have allowed demons to enter. The promiscuous person in his or her 30s certainly has opened the door for more demonic entries than a teenager who is sleeping around. In a word, the older person has a lot more evil conduct to live down and more immoral baggage to shed. Perhaps most critically, the older person has been through more trauma and has more soul wounds to heal. There might be more entrenchment of negative emotions as a result, such as bitterness, lack of forgiveness, anger, rejection, and so on.

God certainly is able to overcome all these difficulties, but the deliverance minister should be aware of the challenges ahead. Remember the importance of the will of the individual seeking

older people are more set in their ways and habits more soul ties and baggage; needs healing from tramas.

Must have the will to be delivered

help. Casting out demons isn't about the man or woman of God overpowering the evil. Deliverance is a collaborative process that involves the deliverance minister agreeing with the fully committed will of the one seeking freedom. If the latter is reluctant in any way, the minister can't complete the process. The case of the Syrophoenician woman in Matthew 15:21–28 demonstrates the role of personal conviction in the journey to deliverance. ("O woman, great is your faith.") Whatever the ages of the people involved, there must be complete unanimity among those resisting the forces of evil, especially from the one seeking help.

Residency Location

This may seem like a strange factor to consider, but the culture of each geographical location affects a person's way of seeing the spirit world. In the United States, a so-called Bible-belt believer might have too much "religion" to see spiritual activity in stark terms. They often have a more casual attitude about spiritual warfare since religion has been so commonplace throughout their life. They could have an "Isn't everyone saved?" attitude (and therefore conclude that they can't have demons) so that they don't take spiritual warfare quite so seriously. On the other hand, a person from the Pacific Northwest might have picked up by cultural osmosis some eclectic ideas about spirituality that syncretize Christian and New Age beliefs. An Angelino who has lived close to Hollywood and cultural liberalism could consider demons as part of some movie special effects gimmick. A New Englander might have absorbed a lot of religious skepticism or universalism.

Yes, I am stroking with a broad brush, but once again generalities can help guide the process of prayer.

For people who come from outside of America, the context of spiritual understanding will differ depending on whether they come from South America (inclined to belief because of the Catholic culture), Asia (very open to the activity of good and evil spirits), or Africa (the most spiritually aware people whose cultures are laden with ancestor and idol worship).

Occupation

Can an individual's daily work involvement affect the degree of demonization? Absolutely. It profoundly affects how a person views the world. Once the deliverance process begins, everything gets filtered through the personal qualities of the prayer recipient and how he or she thinks. For example, artistic people such as musicians or designers will be more likely to see spirits or hear their voices. They may have visionary experiences during the deliverance because their brains are more wired to the paranormal. It's good to have such individuals engage in their own deliverance, as they will be more emotive toward the demons. Conversely, I've found that engineers, lawyers, doctors, and such are a bit more difficult to deal with. They think in linear terms and are accustomed to dealing with hard facts and proven criteria. They are usually less sensitive to interaction with their own deliverance. To them, it's more about the process than it is about their internal psyche.

Education

Believe it or not, this is a profound factor in deliverance. When a demon invades a person, that evil spirit is somewhat captive to the mental processes of the host. Consequently, the more educated a person is, the more sophisticated the demonization and, generally, the harder to dislodge. More educated people are usually thinkers. They operate in their heads more, as a result of their schooling, especially if they went beyond undergraduate level. On a positive note they may be more likely to assist with deductive conclusions about their condition because they have been trained to think that way. However, their minds can get in the way if they are trying to think themselves free. Less educated people tend to accept things as they are without a lot of introspection. That's good up to a point, since it's less likely to interfere with what the deliverance minister wants to do. The drawback is the lack of insightful thinking since they haven't had to challenge their brains as much.

There are always exceptions to these generalizations. Lack of education could be due to financial considerations and yet the person has no less intellectual capacity simply because of never having had the chance to succeed in school. But as a rule, the more the education, the more the direct involvement of the recipient of deliverance, and the greater chance he or she will also intellectually interfere.

Marital Status

If a person is married, and if that marriage is healthy, should such facts have a bearing on getting free from Satan? Whether or not they should, they do. If someone has a good marriage, great. One less issue to resolve. If a 30- or 40-something person is not married, why not? Perhaps the single state was a rational choice. Maybe it was a reaction to abuse in childhood or fear of rejection. You need to find out if the reason for singleness is healthy or reactive.

How many marriages? Multiple marriages may signal a difficulty with bonding or may stem from past trauma that intruded into relationships. Usually, emotionally healthy people choose mates who are similar. The choice of a dysfunctional partner may indicate severe dysfunction in the person seeking deliverance. You must also consider factors of dysfunctional enabling or codependency with a mate. Once you determine the approximate cause for an unhealthy marital state, next you must decide if that is a significant factor where demonization is concerned.

Extended Family

Each of us has been raised in some kind of family structure, for better or for worse. Interaction with siblings, cousins, aunts, uncles, and so forth may greatly affect how a person picks up demons and what kind of demons they are. Did they get along well with brothers and sisters, or was there friction? Difficulties may signal issues of rejection and long-term anger. Worse yet, was there any incest, an all-too-common evil that almost always leads to demonic possession? Were other family members afflicted with addictions to drugs or alcohol? Did these addictions pollute the family structure? Were bloodline relatives involved in any form of the occult? This could lead to powerful curses. As I teach thoroughly in our International School of Exorcism and my book *Curse Breaking,* curses extend not only chronologically (back through the ancestral bloodline), but they also can have a transgenerational effect, extending throughout the living relatives and siblings like a contagion. Determining what evil exists in the extended family is one of the largest fingerprints to look for.

Ethnicity

Racial and ancestral profiling, whether or not it's "PC," is certainly crucial to discovering the dimensions of demonization.

Just knowing the country a person is from or where his or her ancestors originally lived tells a lot. Every racial identity and every ethnic group has its own set of demon issues. Whether a person's background is Nordic, Aryan, European, African, or Hispanic, for example, can telegraph information about the kinds of demons he or she may have. Once again, our International School of Exorcism and my book *Curse Breaking* explain these factors in detail, so there's no need to repeat that material here. Just know that the ethnic make-up of the individual seeking deliverance reveals a lot about the *potential* forms of demonization and the curses that need to be broken before proceeding with the deliverance process.

Cultural Identity

The cultural identity of an individual might actually be different from his or her ethnic identity. I once ministered to an Indian man who lived in Norway but did business in the Caribbean. He had the Hindu demon Kali (India), the Norse demon Thor (Norway), and the strange-sounding name of an African deity (African witchcraft transported to the Islands). The person ministered to might be living in a Slavic country but have roots in Ireland and have picked up Eastern European demons from superstition he adopted living in the former Soviet Union. He might be Caucasian from the American Midwest but doing business in Japan. Along the way he got Buddhist demons by going to temple ceremonies and investigating that religious system to help him relate better to locals.

Religious History

What religious faiths a person may have encountered in life will certainly affect his or her understanding of having an exorcism.

As an example, consider the issues of dealing with generational curses. The reality of generational curses is resisted by the majority of evangelical Christians in America. Not so, once you leave our shores. In most of the Caribbean, South and Central America, Africa, India, Asia, and the Far East such teachings are readily accepted. This is because America has enjoyed the benefits of roughly 400 years of Christian culture. Historically, no one has had to deliver most Americans from tribalism, idolatry, and ancestor worship, although that is rapidly changing with the influx of the New Age and Eastern religions.

There are essentially four uniquely American theological adaptations that resist the idea of inheriting evil from one's ancestors. This subject is covered thoroughly in my book *Curse Breaking*. I'm not suggesting that these viewpoints automatically deny the reality of generational sins, but a misreading of these doctrinal viewpoints has led many to deny bloodline evil. If people seeking deliverance come from one of these perspectives, or have been raised in a home where this was strongly taught, their deliverance might be impeded.

1. *Reformed/Calvinist.* If one is predestined to be either blessed or cursed, then the choices of evil ancestors have no bearing. An individual's spiritual standing with God is a matter of election and sovereign design, and therefore predisposed tendencies to evil are irrelevant.

2. *Wesleyan/Holiness.* If one is fully sanctified by a "second work of grace," there can be no place for generational curses to abide. All inherited evil tendencies are eradicated.

3. *Anabaptist/Baptist.* An incorrect view of the "once saved, always saved" view has caused many pastors to teach that beyond salvation there can be nothing left of original sin or inherited iniquities.

4. *Pentecostal/charismatic.* If speaking in tongues is the sign of the fullness of the Spirit's presence, then the presence of this spiritual gift means that one who is "filled" cannot have anything else abiding within, spiritually or genetically.

Current Religious Affiliation

The present religious mindset of an individual seeking deliverance is also crucial. I once spent more than an hour with a person who was asking for ministry before he told me that he didn't believe a Christian could have a demon. It was what his church taught, and he wasn't backing down from that belief. To seek help from an exorcist under those circumstances seemed a clear contradiction to me, but not to him. I learned my lesson well and now always find out the theological mindset of the person receiving ministry. On occasion I've discovered that someone seeking help is part of a cult-like group, and ministry isn't possible until that spiritual soul tie is broken. I don't always theologically agree with everyone who needs deliverance, and that is OK. What I don't want is a hidden doctrinal agenda that clutters what I am trying to do by undercutting the steps to freedom I'm advising. Knowing that possibility in advance is better than trying to decipher it later in the heat of spiritual battle with demonic forces.

BACK TO THE HOLLERS

What about Edna? The more I talked with her, the more her story fit a pattern; but a surprise was still in store for me.

Let's break down her case by the criteria above:

1.   *Age*. Older, so whatever demons she had might be difficult to dislodge.

2.   *Residency location*. Though she now lived in a large city, her mind and emotions were still back in the poverty-ridden, culturally stunted confines of her youth. The demons could use that disconnected mindset to their advantage, feeding off the despair she'd have felt decades ago.

3.   *Occupation*. None. Totally dependent upon her husband. Not a good situation. More feelings of helplessness to overcome.

4.   *Education*. This wasn't in her favor. I could tell she was instinctively bright, but had no higher education. Her demons wouldn't be mind-control types, but more likely emotionally related spirits taking advantage of her limited opportunities.

5.   *Marital status*. Not good, obviously. She was married to a man she loathed and was only there out of obligation.

6.   *Extended family*. She didn't know. Once they had a chance to escape their sad surroundings,

they all split for parts unknown. No help with that one to better understand how her three siblings fared.

7. *Ethnicity.* Who knew? That wasn't anything people in her community cared about or talked about. Caucasian was all we could generally determine.

8. *Cultural identity.* As I've already pointed out, her impoverished and socially deprived environment could lead to a sense of shame and isolation later in life, as well as a feeling that nothing was ever going to change. Her people mostly never escaped their situations. At least Edna had made it to the "big city."

9. *Religious history.* As already stated, hers was a quite provincial and legalistic background laden with lots of rules and false expectations. Not much theological depth, but a whole lot of guilt.

10. *Current religious affiliation.* At last, a bright spot. She attended a thriving church and accepted the reality of spiritual warfare and deliverance. They would embrace her newfound freedom and encourage her to go deeper in God.

+ The final analysis? Not much likelihood of exotic demons of cross-cultural significance. Her ancestors were pretty isolated. The main problem seemed to be her lack of having had available resources to turn to in order to get out of her predicament. No big generational issues seemed to be looming, except the barefoot-and-pregnant approach to her spousal role. What I did note was a form of spiritual abuse. It seems no one in her religious community thought it outrageous that this mere child would marry someone almost old enough to be her father and be forced into sexual servitude. This had the spirit of Jezebel written all over it because of the sexual abuse of corrupted religion. Edna's confinement in a long-term marriage of duty rather than emotional nurturing meant that spirits of Anger and Bitterness were also likely at work. I didn't expect to deal with Occultism or Witchcraft, but Depression and Suicide had to be there somewhere. Her age might normally make this code tough to crack, but her internalized rage at years of mistreatment could blow things wide open. Presumably, by now the reader can understand how my mental processes broke down the components of Edna's demonization.

"Jezebel, I know you're there. I call you to judgment," I shouted.

Great-Grandma lunged for me, and alert, strong men quickly grabbed her before she could do any harm. Demonized people can have supernatural strength, so her age was no comfort to me.

"What do you want?" the demon screamed. "I've had her all these years, and I'm not leaving."

Demons always say that. I quickly informed them that wasn't the case and began the roll call based on my deductions.

"Bitterness? Anger?"

"Yeah, we're here too. And don't forget Rage."

"Of course, I expected him."

"Suicide, too. You know we've almost got her to the point of giving up...if you hadn't come along. Why do you always mess up our plans?"

"I don't, Jesus does," I responded.

The demons smirked in disgust. "It won't be as easy as you think to get rid of us," they challenged. They were right.

We battled these evil forces with prayer, Scripture reading, and rebuke for nearly an hour. I realized we must be missing something—or someone. Then, the Holy Spirit revealed to me…

"Lilith, that's who's at the top. That's the Strong Man."

Edna erupted into her most violent reaction yet. She wasn't exactly spry, but you'd never know it the way her legs shot out from under her to kick me. The men who held her were sweating and struggling to keep her from breaking loose. It was Lilith, all right, the one I call "Jezebel on steroids," a super-version of Jezebel.

Students of our School of Exorcism and readers of my book *Jezebel* know all about Lilith, the demon who claims to be Adam's real wife before supposedly being kicked out by Eve, whom occultists believe sexually seduced Adam to replace Lilith.

The code had been cracked. The battle had been won and in minutes the war for Edna's soul was over as Lilith, Jezebel, and all the rest were sent packing back to hell!

No amount of prayer assault, boisterous shouting, laying on of hands, or any other "traditional" approach to deliverance would have worked in this case. Edna's freedom required patience, careful observation, asking the right questions, and patiently following the trail of fingerprints left by Satan.

PERSPECTIVE

The medical and scientific communities have accepted norms for establishing and approving how their professions will be practiced. Oddly, the more important area of spiritual warfare ministry, which has eternal consequences, is all too often done in a capricious manner, lacking in discipline. To counter that unqualified attitude toward deliverance ministry, this chapter suggests that when helping those who are demonically bound, two principles need to be followed: (1) The deliverance minister should be constantly looking for the fingerprint of Satan, evidence of the devil's interference, and (2) he or she should also be aware of ways to crack the code of the devil's finely tuned plans of killing, stealing, and destroying all that is good.

In most cases, before any attempt is made to confront demonic forces and expel them, a lot of homework needs to be done. I suggested earlier in this chapter at least ten areas to be probed for signs that the devil is at work in someone's life. This approach shouldn't be engaged in mechanically, checking off each area one by one like a doctor asking a patient to list all past surgeries and current medications. The approach to these ten crucial areas of information should be fluid, with the information evolving as inquiries are made and conversation ensues. Clients shouldn't feel that they are being systematically processed. Rather, these matters of concern should be woven into a fabric of inquiry that expresses loving concern for the plight of the suffering soul. Nevertheless, the deliverance minister needs to keep a list of all these critical facts so that spiritual weaknesses and deficiencies can be quickly spotted.

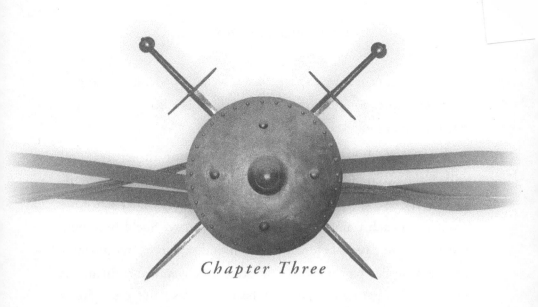

Chapter Three

THE FINGERPRINT
OF THE FAMILY

BEFORE OUR INTERNATIONAL SCHOOL OF EXORCISM CURRICULUM was translated into various languages, I would regularly hold foreign conferences to accommodate those wanting to learn our techniques of dealing with the devil. One such training took place annually in Ukraine. There, hundreds of interested students from more than 20 nations including ROOussia, Siberia, Scandinavia, Europe, and other Slavic countries gathered.

One day while teaching about the influence of family dynamics on spiritual oppression, a tall Lithuanian woman stood and began to shout in Russian. A torrent of emotion was obviously pouring forth, though I had no idea what her words actually meant. At first she seemed to be venting some deeply repressed feeling of frustration, but as she continued to speak, her words turned bitterly angry; then her expression was openly demonic as her body shook from whatever had provoked the evil spirits in her.

I approached her, commanded the demons to regress, and called the woman to full consciousness. Her name was Mariana. Forty-five years of age. Single now, but thrice married. One child from each union and a fourth illegitimate. She'd become a Christian three years before and was attending our exorcism training because her pastor wanted to start a deliverance team in his church. After gathering these few basic facts (as I suggested doing in chapter two), I set out to probe her more thoroughly about how she had been raised. The fingerprint of the family can often be the most significant source of information in any form of counseling or psychotherapy. In deliverance ministry, it is indispensable.

THE FINGERPRINT OF THE FATHER

"First, tell me about your father," I said to Mariana.

"I was a child during Soviet times, before the fall of the Communist Empire and the end of its control over Eastern Europe. Things were rough, but we survived somehow. Lithuania was a difficult place to live in in the 1980s."

I had ministered before to many people of Eastern Europe raised during Soviet subjugation. I could almost anticipate what Mariana was going to say. The story was a familiar one. Through my Russian interpreter, she described her childhood.

"Papa worked hard. And drank hard. Days at the factory were long and without much personal satisfaction." She lowered her head. "Sometimes he had too much vodka and would come home to beat me...or my mother. We understood. It wasn't him; it was the alcohol. He really loved me. I know he did. He just didn't say it."

Tears streamed down her cheeks, and she trembled from the old emotions of her earliest years. "I'm sure he must have loved me. I loved him, even when..."

The pause was painful. "...he grabbed my mother by the hair and dragged her across the room. I guess the hardest part was seeing blood streaming out of my mother's nose and mouth from where he'd hit her."

Mariana collapsed into her chair and doubled over in convulsing sobs.

My exploration of her past wasn't finished yet, but one strong ridge of her family's fingerprint was apparent: she had been raised by a drunken, cruel father who was trapped by the times in which he lived and no one had any recourse for spiritual help when atheism enforced every facet of life.

What did strike me was something that I'd heard before from those who grew up in a home of domestic violence: what I call personal, historical revisionism. They quite literally rewrite their past.

HINDSIGHT BIAS

I am indebted to author Joseph T. Hallinan for his books *Why We Make Mistakes*. The book is primarily an exploration of the human condition of error, even with the best of intentions and meticulousness in avoiding it. In the section of his book called "Hindsight Isn't Twenty-Twenty," Hallinan points out that "hindsight bias" is a constant source of human error. In essence, the author believes that the outcome of individuals' lives has a strong influence on how they see the past. This is what he calls "hindsight bias."

Almost every person I have counseled who experienced tragedy at a young age has such bias. What a person becomes later in life affects how they remember what it was like many years before. This is the historical revisionism I referred to. Many times a retrospective lens on the past ought not to be trusted. Our emotions lie to us, especially if demonic forces are there to reinforce that lie. I've seen this play out over and over. The result is that people coming for ministry may not be able to recognize curses in their past because the evil that was said or done to them has been so greatly minimized.

The victim of any kind of childhood abuse or mistreatment has a vested interest in hindsight bias. It aids their ability to overlook how terrible past experiences may have been. The upside is it may ameliorate some of the effect of significant trauma. The downside is that it covers up painful memories that need to be healed. More than that, it actually rewrites the way that those memories are perceived, placing them in a less horrific context. Hindsight bias is one thing if it's a matter of how a historian views a past war or the effect of a certain political regime. It's another matter if the bias conceals or minimizes the effect of personal evil on the one who has experienced it. This concealment is one way that demonic forces keep a tormented individual from seeking help. They so negate the authenticity of their emotions that they actually lie to themselves about the truth of what happened.

Creeping Determinism

Hallinan also points out another concept that is important in ministering to those who have been demonically attacked:

"creeping determinism." Not only are human beings prone to exaggerate or minimize past occurrences, depending on the particular need, but they also "misremember" what actually happened. In my words, they lie to themselves. Note again that demons may be part of this process of prevarication. The effect is even more dramatic if the individual also suffered something so terrible that there was an immediate need to cancel its pain by instantly reframing the event in the mind. This is why in deliverance ministry the process of inner healing and recovered memories is so important. So is exploring the possibility of dissociative identity disorder (DID). More about that later.

Back to Mariana. Notice how she, in just a few words, spoke of her past. It's common for victims of abuse to make excuses about the bad behavior of their abuser, especially a parent. In this case the tormentor was Mariana's father. She so wanted to love her father (as she wished he had been) that hindsight bias kicked in. In addition, as a Christian she was motivated by the forgiveness ethic that "love covers a multitude of sins" (see 1 Peter 4:8). Shouldn't she give grace to her father and see the best in him to overlook his drunken rages? That's the mind-game that many Christians play in their attitude toward past abusers. It sounds good, but it's a deadly trap laid by evil spirits. A lie is a lie, no matter what extenuating circumstances may be present. When that lie is at the root of a demonic opening in one's life, such as Mariana's shading the account of her father's brutality, the outcome is always the same: continued bondage until the truth comes through and can be faced honestly.

In Mariana's case, I took a few moments to role-play with her. I assumed the role of her father and asked her to look directly at me and say how she felt about the unacceptable actions of her father.

At first she hesitated, averting her eyes and, mumbling something about how sad she was as a child.

I interrupted. I spoke harshly to get her attention. "What do you really think about how I treated you and your mother?" I did my best to project the demeanor of her father. It provoked her.

Mariana now fixed her eyes on me. My directness had jolted something inside her. I could sense her anger rising. Her eyes flared. He body tensed. Her lips trembled. Then she exploded.

"My life today is a disaster because of you. My first husband beat me just as you did Mom. My second husband cheated over and over until I couldn't take it anymore and left. My third husband was a drunk like you. I and the kids never knew when we'd be out on the street. I'll never find love. I wish I could die. It didn't have to be like this, but you made it this way. YOU! You were a monster. I'm tired of blaming everything else, even myself, for how you treated us. The worst part was watching my mother slowly lose her mind until she lived in a fantasy world of mental illness."

Mariana was so much into the moment that she stepped toward me and began pounding my chest with her fists. At that moment, I was her father, the man she had never given herself permission to be angry with, all those years. Suddenly, she wasn't the one wrong anymore. In a few brief moments, her hindsight bias took a back seat to the truth of what her real emotions told her.

Then she collapsed to her knees, bent forward, sobbing tears that had been pent up for more than 30 years. She wasn't delivered yet from her demons, but she had taken the first step toward her healing. Her father had been fingerprinted.

THE MATRIX OF THE MOTHER

Using Mariana as an example, let's explore how a mother's fingerprint also affects what becomes of an individual's life.

As I said earlier, when I begin ministering to someone, whether in a confrontational exorcism or in a more sedate counseling setting, I always want to know everything possible about the family dynamics. Each case is different, and I only use Mariana as an example to illustrate the way such an understanding works. Every individual's personal history is different. Good and bad parenting skills and the tragic presence of neglect or abuse must be factored in. What's significant is discovering all the consequential influences on a child's life that could have facilitated demonic oppression.

Mothers are nurturers by nature. When nurture is absent in a home, whether due to willful withholding or a dysfunctional marital relationship, the deleterious effect is immense. Obviously, Mariana's mother was an enabler. We can excuse her failure in many ways. She was part of a patriarchal culture in which women had little say. Life under Soviet rule was often reduced to mere survival, and she likely had few economic options for escape. She may have even believed the lie that her husband really loved her and that he'd change someday. Or she may have felt it her duty to endure, because her life in those days, under those circumstances, might have been even more tragic minus a man in the house.

Whatever the rationale for a mother in such a situation, none of the extenuating circumstances matter to a child. The effect of the mother-matrix in which a youth is raised shapes his or her life. In fact, it is a basic psychological rule that the self-perceptive identity of children is formed by the age of three, and most certainly by the middle to late childhood years. The self-sentient way in which they define their individuality comes primarily from the family—or the lack of one, in cases of abandonment or severe neglect. Therefore, knowing how a mother did or did not treat a child is crucial to understanding one of the ways that evil operates.

Mariana's mother had put her at risk, both physically and emotionally. No matter that such circumstances might have been somewhat unavoidable. All the things Mariana needed from her mother were absent: safety, positive emotional reinforcement, a listening ear, comfort, and most of all, spiritual guidance. Furthermore, her parents, both individually and together, gave their daughter no emotional tools for finding a life partner. She married what she was familiar with: callousness, rancor, narcissism.

Mariana's case was extreme. However, I've encountered much, much worse. But as a case in point it shows what happens when a mother deliberately or unknowingly fails in some way to carry out her God-given responsibilities.

An important word of advice. When you ask people how they were raised by their mother or father, be aware that children have no comparative context by which to measure the emotional and spiritual health of their upbringing. In most cases, there were no other options or models to observe. Children often assume that what happens in their home is "normal," no matter how aberrant it may be. Their only reference point is what went on behind their four walls. In ministering healing and deliverance, wrong assumptions about home life must often be challenged.

Why? The truth about Mom and Dad can't be whitewashed. The suffering child, now an adult, can't truly forgive with emotional integrity until the damage from bad parenting is recognized. Here is a simple spiritual rule that I've discovered: clemency demands an acknowledgment of guilt; pardon means having first issued a guilty verdict. The child from a damaging home life must mentally indict the bad behavior that resulted in his or her spiritual bondage. Then that child can truly experience the fullness of forgiveness.

THE FINGERPRINT OF SIBLINGS

When I begin the deliverance process of prayer I usually first want to know not only about how parents raised the person receiving ministry, but also about his or her interaction with siblings. How many? Boys or girls? Was there any bullying or rivalry fringing on physical violence? Worse yet, any sexual abuse?

And this is important. How did the other siblings turn out? Are they relationally and spiritually successful? Are there any consistent patterns of dysfunction that might indicate a family curse common to all siblings? The life-success or failure of brothers and sisters may reveal underlying problems in the home that even the person you are praying with might not have recognized.

Here are some of the patterns, fingerprints, I often encounter: multiple divorces, addictions, difficulty with relational bonding, spiritual anemia, anger issues, difficulties with parenting. In a family of perhaps four or five children, it's not unusual for one or two to go bad. But the accounts I hear are often worse. In some cases, none or few of the siblings have attained personal success. It's not an issue of someone in the brood being a black sheep; I often hear that *all* the siblings turned out badly. This is often a clear indicator of demonic interference and unbroken generational curses.

It's helpful to search for the common factors that sabotaged all the siblings. What have the majority of the brothers and sisters in the family struggled with? Broken marriages?

Addictions to drugs or alcohol? Failure to financially succeed despite educational opportunities?

THE EXPANDED FINGERPRINT OF THE FAMILY

There are still more questions to ask about the health of the organic family structure:

- Did Mom and Dad stay together?

- If the parents divorced, what happened next? Remarriage? How many times?

- If the marriage dissolved, why? Was unfaithfulness a factor?

- Was the respondent raised by a stepparent? How well did that go?

- If extreme dysfunction was evident, did it result in being raised in any foster family?

- How close are family members today?

What are we looking for? Patterns. Symptomatic signs of demonic interference. Instances of being at risk for sexual abuse. Circumstances leading to feelings of rejection, abandonment, or both. When all the identifiable signs point to dysfunctional family systems, there is no way the respondent can convince me that his or her childhood was all "Beaver Cleaver." If there is sufficient indication of more than normal adversity, I know there is a code to crack, and I shift from my concerned and compassionate mind to my forensic mode. I keep asking questions until I hit on something that, in the spiritual universe, has significance.

Example. The person I'm helping insists he had a good home and fine Christian parents. But further investigation reveals that the parents split shortly after the individual graduated from high school. Dad moved in with another woman soon after. Mom remarried a few years later, a short-term relationship that also ended in divorce. Of the person's three siblings, only one sister is still walking with the Lord; one sister is on her third marriage and a brother struggles with alcohol. Neither of the dysfunctional siblings attends church. And this was a loving, Christian home? Hindsight bias may have wished that it were, but reality says something else. And that something else left open a number of invitations for demonic entrance and attachment.

Is it possible that there is some inherited evil behind all of these failed lives? It's clear that in any dysfunctional family system each flawed individual makes personally unhealthy choices. But has some generational X-factor pushed things further in wrong directions, making things worse than they might have been?

As I have mentioned already, I have written a lengthy, detailed book on curses, so I will not repeat that information here. And while our International School of Exorcism teaches in depth how generational curses operate and the many ways they afflict descendants, also consider the following information which is not contained in my book, due to the more recent nature of its disclosure.

CRACKING THE GENETIC CODE OF CURSES

In spite of the testimony of church history and theology, plus the witness of thousands of ministers of deliverance, the concept of generational curses still meets resistance from mainstream American evangelicalism. In other parts of the world, such as

Africa, this idea is more or less accepted. Cultures which are but a few generations removed from idolatrous practices recognize that the bloodline carries powerful proclivities toward evil which are spiritually embedded and must be removed. Paradoxically, if some Christian pastors won't yield to the obvious evidence, psychology and science may come to the rescue.

Epigenetics is a new study of how the factors of one's environment can actually change a person's DNA, and that these alterations can be inherited! In August of 2015, the journal *Biological Psychiatry* published a study of Holocaust survivors and their adult children.[1] According to the study, high stress releases hormones called glucocorticoids. Continued exposure to these hormones eventually reduces an individual's ability to handle trauma. The hormones turn off certain genes which would normally handle stress. In other words, the effects of severe trauma have a powerful impact on the sufferer's actual DNA, a condition which then affects the ability of future generations to handle difficulties. One generation's maladies can become the next generation's emotional hindrances. We're talking science and genetics here; researchers with no interest one way or another in proving that curses can be passed on to offspring, which is what Scripture has taught for millennia!

As cases in point, researchers found that the daughters of Dutch women who were pregnant during a famine after World War II had an above-average risk of developing schizophrenia. From what those of us in deliverance know about inner healing, we see the same thing happen to victims of emotional, physical, and sexual abuse. Clearly, demons understand the effect of glucocorticoids and take advantage of the vulnerable in successive generations.

Thus, for example, a victim of childhood sexual abuse who doesn't receive counseling and spiritual healing may over-secrete these hormones which alter DNA, a modification which may be passed on to the children. The children could then suffer depression and various mental illnesses and consequently be more vulnerable to sexual abuse themselves. And this mutated pattern could continue for many generations until the curse is spiritually broken and God supernaturally modifies the DNA.

According to Lee Bitsoi, PhD, Research Associate in Genetics at Harvard University, epigenetic changes may be linked to the "development of illnesses such as PTSD, depression, and type 2 diabetes."[2] The findings of Bitsoi have been extended to high rates of addiction, suicide, and sexual violence. This Harvard researcher is saying exactly what I've declared in my book *Curse Breaking*.

PERSPECTIVE

The evil that happens to one generation is transferable to the next. Demons know this and stalk the vulnerable, attacking them with various mental, emotional, and physical problems. And though science may come up with drugs to counter the damage of glucocorticoids, prayer to break curses is an important form of immediate intervention that must not be overlooked by Christians. My book *Curse Breaking* includes 25 pages of detailed curse-breaking prayers that confront hundreds of infirmities, psychological difficulties, and spiritual impediments. Critics of curse-breaking need to be better informed before they pass harsh judgments on those of us who every day see the effects of generational curses, and who also witness the power of Christ to cancel all the evil committed by bloodline ancestors.

The family, God's basic building block of civilization, is where the best and the worst of nobility and evil is fostered. Finding the fingerprint of past generational evil and deciphering the contaminated imprint of the current family structure are vital to the process of dealing with demons.

NOTES

1. See abstract at http://www.biologicalpsychiatryjournal. com/article/S0006-3223(15)00652-6/abstract and article at http://www.theguardian.com/science/2015/aug/21/study -of-holocaust-survivors-finds-trauma-passed-on-to -childrens-genes.

2. Kit O'Connell, "Native Americans Have 'Always Known': Science Proves Genetic Inheritance of Trauma," on Shadowproof.com (https://shadowproof.com/2015/08/27/ native-americans-have-always-known-science-proves-genetic -inheritance-of-trauma/).

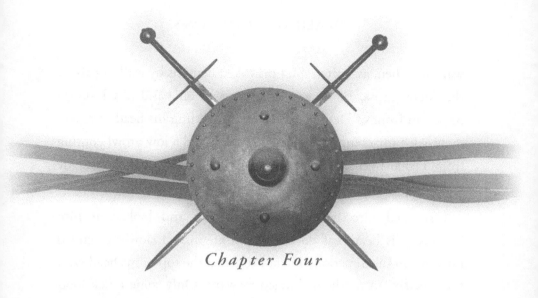

Chapter Four

THE GOD FACTOR

DENNIS LOVED GOD. AGED 42, HE WAS A DEVOTED FAMILY MAN. His three young children doted on him. He worked hard and provided well for his family. It was, by all outside observations, a well-oiled Christian home, except for Dennis's occasional, angry outbursts. They were volatile, but short-lived. No one close to him ever suspected that his behavior might be demonic in origin. First, Dennis was a Christian, and the conventional wisdom of his spiritual peers dismissed any idea of demonic influence on his conduct. Second, he came from a long generational line of believers. At least it seemed that way.

Then Dennis came to one of my seminars. He sat in the front row, all the better to get a good look at what might happen. I taught, exhorted, encouraged, and instructed the audience in spiritual warfare. Then, as I often do, I provoked demons by walking about the room, cross, Bible, and anointing oil in hand. As I slowly passed in front of Dennis, who'd been nodding his head in agreement with my comments all night, I detected a low growl coming from inside him. Without wanting to tip my hand, I casually strode by him again. The growl grew louder.

I stopped directly in front of Dennis and looked at him intently. His head was down as if in anguish. I slowly extended my cross in his direction. Then, I touched the top of his head with the crucifix. Instantly, he lunged forward. Only some quick footwork on my part prevented me from being knocked over. Dennis was now flat on his stomach. The growl turned into a scream. He thrashed about violently. Thankfully, a half dozen strong men ran from every corner of the room and grabbed any appendage they could to control Dennis. The mayhem that followed sent people seated near Dennis scurrying. Before calm could be restored, ten men were either hanging on to an arm or leg or were piled on top of him. All this to subdue a man far short of six feet and likely not more than 150–160 pounds. What could possibly have caused such a violent outburst?

I cautiously approached Dennis and asked the men holding him to release their grip. Dazed and confused by what had happened, Dennis slowly stood to his feet, wondering why, when he came to consciousness, he was smothered by what resembled a rugby scrum. When I briefly recounted the events that lead to his being piled on by hundreds of pounds of manpower, he shook his head in disbelief. But with hundreds of people watching and affirming what had happened, there was no disputing my account.

Following the protocol laid out in the first three chapters of this book, I gathered a few basic facts about his situation. Then

I focused on his spiritual life. He was a Christian, the born-again variety, saved at 15 at a church camp. He regularly attended church and tithed scrupulously. He was active in a Bible study that met weekly. It all sounded good, but something was not quite right. But what? The contradiction was between his actions now and what he seemed to profess before this night.

"So, tell me about that camp," I asked.

"It was Baptist, and the church was down the street from my house," Dennis explained. "I went there with friends until I got older. Then I started going to a Pentecostal church. I liked the music and services that were more lively. But..."

He hesitated for a moment. "But what?"

"They believed things that were a lot different from the Baptist church where I was saved. I guess I always felt conflicted about both groups being Christian but being so far apart on things like speaking in tongues and whether I could lose my salvation." He stopped to think for a moment. "Something inside me keeps thinking that with such huge differences that maybe this whole Christian thing might not be the real deal after all."

As he said that I detected a faint demonic glee in his eyes. I knew I was on to something, both in the mind of Dennis and in the hidden evil of his ancestors. But that would have to be flushed out, somewhat painstakingly.

I've done thousands of exorcisms in public forums across decades of ministry. I could have easily gone forward with Dennis, but I sensed that his case was going to be too complicated for a quick resolution. I suggested that we meet the next day in a more relaxed, private setting where I could pick apart his mind without pressing time constraints.

Dealing with demons isn't always about direct, bombastic confrontation. It's often like a delicate spiritual chess match, with lots of potential checkmates to be overcome. Sometimes Satan's strongholds are found in subtle issues about belief, doctrine, even eschatology. The reader who comes from a more typical perspective on deliverance might be thinking, "Why all this bother? Just get on with it and get out the demons like Jesus did."

Really? And just how did Jesus cast out demons? His approach with the demon Legion in chapter 8 of Luke was much different from the demon-possessed man in the synagogue, found in the first chapter of Mark. In fact, the account of the Syrophoenician woman in the seventh chapter of Mark illustrates the important role faith plays in being set free. That instance was not at all instantaneous and consisted of an evolving dialogue between Christ and this mother of a demon-possessed daughter. I suppose that Jesus, being God incarnate, could have immediately spoken a word and rectified the situation, but He didn't. Only after drawing out this Canaanite woman's thinking about spiritual intervention did Jesus finally declare, "The demon has gone out of your daughter" (Mark 7:29). Jesus needed to make plain to the woman and all who were watching (as well as those reading Scripture) that what a person believes is a crucial component in the process of being freed from demons. He first tested her faith and then delivered her daughter.

THE ANATOMY OF BELIEF AND ITS EFFECT

So, what did I discover in further conversation with Dennis that next day? Five important facts:

First, Dennis was performance-oriented in his relationship with Christ. The theological confusion he experienced, being saved one place but worshiping in another, left him feeling confused about who was really right. His emotionally internalized solution was to please God by being good enough. That way, he could be sure to "stay saved" no matter what was happening inside his head. That subtle lack of faith by grace was enough for demons to exploit.

Second, at the true spiritual core of his belief system was the idea that either being baptized as a Baptist or speaking in tongues as a Pentecostal would hedge his bets about who might be right in eternal terms. In other words, what mattered wasn't what he *really* believed (whichever way he might have leaned) but rather playing the percentages. A small thing? Sure, but as you'll see later in this chapter, there were generational issues unbeknownst to Dennis that were cleverly exploiting the slightest chink in his spiritual armor.

Third, the dilemma of Dennis went much deeper than Anabaptist doctrine versus an Arminian approach to the security of the believer. Dennis actually wondered deep inside how he could have been redeemed in the first place if the personal moral issues he struggled with couldn't be resolved. From the time he first looked at pornography at age seven, Dennis had periodically given in to lust, even in his current "godly" marriage. Would a saved person act that way? Maybe that camp conversion was just so much emotion at a vulnerable time in his young life. In this way the devil was planting serous doubt that he was a Christian after all.

Then there was the issue of whether a Christian could even have a demon. To the Baptist side of his brain, it was an irrelevant issue. They never talked about demons or ever mentioned anything like deliverance. It was a moot matter. The Pentecostals gave lip service to the idea of deliverance, but Dennis couldn't remember if they'd ever actually done an exorcism on anyone.

What they did do was rail against the idea that a Christian might be demonized, considering that the mere mention of the possibility was rank heresy. If someone seeming to be a Christian exhibited demonic behavior, well then, the explanation was simple. They had somehow lost their salvation to get the demon. Case closed.

All this theological point-counterpoint left Dennis emotionally numb. But there was yet one more dark secret lurking in Dennis's mind. He had heard indirectly that his father may have been unfaithful to his mother. Dad was a deacon at church. He passed the offering baskets and greeted people with a smile as they entered the sanctuary. He also served on the church Board of Directors and was looked to for his leadership skills. But at home, things didn't reflect that overt spirituality. Dennis couldn't remember his parents ever praying over the family other than at mealtime. I pushed Dennis to see how relational his upbringing had been. I wasn't surprised by what he told me. Mom and Dad rarely kissed or hugged, and when it did happen, it was perfunctory. They actually slept in separate bedrooms all the while he was growing up. And that pornography he was introduced to at age seven? Magazines found under his dad's bed. There was obviously something "rotten in Denmark," and the demons knew it.

BREAKING DOWN THE GOD FACTOR

How did I sort through all this in order to minister effectively to Dennis? His case in point suggests broader principles for handling investigations about an individual's spiritual life. Here are suggestions I've found helpful:

Theology Is Important

A person's core beliefs are important. And it is crucial to define what those beliefs are, beyond orthodox, non-negotiable doctrines of (1) the nature of God, (2) the Person of Christ, (3) the source of revelation, (4) the state of the fallen human condition, and (5) the hope of redemption and atonement. While it's not necessary that the ministry client have a totally clear understanding of all elements of evangelical doctrine, these core historic beliefs are important for the individual to affirm at some point during the deliverance process. For doctrines and strictures beyond this (such as Dennis's theological struggle), it's not important to determine which is "right," as long as the person receiving ministry is at least reasonably persuaded in some direction.

Don't try to convert the person to your viewpoint. That's doctrinal proselytizing, not necessarily compassionate ministry. Encourage the person at least to be "fully persuaded" in his or her own mind (Romans 14:5, KJV). Confusion or indecision is what demons will exploit. A settled mind, though its conclusions may theologically differ from your views, is more important than a wavering conscience. Demons thrive in a vacuum of indecisiveness. Your goal is not theological conformity but rather a clearly defined belief system so at least you know what the client holds to be true.

Issues of Christian Demonization Must Be Resolved

This is often the 800-pound gorilla in the room that everyone ignores. For those looking for a detailed scriptural resolution of this matter, our International School of Exorcism explores this issue in depth. It is not my purpose here to lay out all the biblical and empirical factors that lead to this conclusion that saved, even Spirit-filled Christians can be indwelt by demons. I have documented more than 40,000 such cases in more than 100 countries of the world. No successful deliverance minister who has a substantial caseload of exorcisms believes Christians can't have demons. Those who hold this position simply don't do deliverance to any extent or not at all. It's a theologically prejudiced conclusion that cannot withstand either serious biblical scrutiny or experiential evidence.

I have performed exorcism on and cast out demons from pastors, priests, nuns, pastor's wives and children, worship leaders, Bible teachers, deacons, elders, etc. These exorcisms have sometimes occurred in public with the entire congregation aware of the identity of the person being exorcised. Family members and church leaders testify to the spiritual faithfulness of such individuals. I could name names, specific actual churches, and cite specific examples. The identities of some Christian leaders out of whom I've cast demons I will take to my grave, never disclosing them for confidential reasons. The reader would recognize the names of some of these individuals were I to reveal them, they are so well-known. Once such person, who had a generational spirit of Murder, attempted to assault me with the intent of bodily harm. Yet this person is a household name in Christian circles. How can that be? Again, I refer you to our exorcism school for more instruction in this controversial area of doctrine.

The important point is that it's nearly impossible to cast demons out of a Christian who has demons and doesn't believe that Christians can have demons.

This is the ultimate paradox in spiritual warfare! I've had many frustrating sessions of dealing with a violent, dangerous case of possession, during which I risked serious personal harm, only to, when I was ready to cast out the demon, have the Christian client's consciousness surface and tell me that he or she couldn't believe there are demons present. All this, even though other witnesses have seen this saved person curse vilely, blaspheme God and Christ, display superhuman strength requiring restraint, and defy good Christian people wanting to help. Such sessions can last hours, and after all the hard and dangerous work has been done, clients opt out because their theology won't accept the reality of being both saved *and* demonized.

Don't Be Drawn into Theological Debates

Christians are very bad about wanting other Christians to believe as they do—*exactly* as they do. Dealing with demons is not about winning a doctrinal debate. It's about bringing hope and healing to those suffering. Will winning an argument about the five points ("TULIP") of Calvinism defeat demons that are there because of childhood sexual abuse? Will convincing someone the fullness of the Holy Spirit is proven only by speaking in tongues eradicate the generational legal rights claimed by a demon of witchcraft? Will believing in the Rapture (or not) break the curse of sorcery for a client who has dabbled in the occult and who has witchcraft in the family bloodline?

Sometimes it's not only the deliverance minister who needs to heed this warning. The client wanting deliverance may want to argue about nonessential aspects of theology. I recall one woman who came for deliverance with a briefcase filled with Bible commentaries and books by her favorite preachers. She spent most of the time I allotted to her trying to convince me that certain things that she *assumed* that I believed were wrong. We never did get around to casting out any demons. She was too busy on her quest to correct me than to look inside herself and see the bondage that was destroying her life.

I'm not saying that doctrine and theology are irrelevant. Not at all. But a time of deliverance prayer when you're dealing with demons isn't the occasion for such discussions. Generals in a war may have different ideas about how to engage the enemy, but in the heat of battle they pick up their guns and start shooting. Dealing with demons is about strategy for spiritual engagement with evil, not an opportunity to examine hermeneutics. When faced with a demonic manifestation, deal with the devil and don't try to resolve superfluous matters in an endless cycle that leaves the enemy unchallenged.

Non-Christians Can Be Delivered

What I'm about to examine is a revolutionary idea in deliverance circles. It's assumed by most people who cast out demons that the person in question must first make a clear confession of faith before you can proceed. It's thought and taught that the demons won't go unless Jesus is there first. At one time I believed this, until the Lord led me into situations with unbelievers where the Holy Spirit directed me to minister first and evangelize later, or sometimes not at all.

Consider this case. A woman who was a devout Buddhist came to me. She was more than devout; she was ardent. She had traveled the world going from one Buddhist site to another, spending much time in India and Tibet. Her quest was to find answers for her constant torment and spiritual attacks. Buddhists believe in malevolent forces, and sometimes actually call them demons. They have elaborate exorcism rituals to rid themselves of these entities. Knowing this, the woman seeking my help had gone to one lama after another with no success. Finally, one Buddhist teacher recommended that she see me. I knew how intensely she followed Buddhism, and that, if I challenged her beliefs, she'd likely walk away without getting help. So I started by talking about what hurt she had experienced in her life.

She painfully spoke of being molested multiple times growing up and then being raped in college. Gradually, I was able to take her to this place of shame which was buried deep inside. When I did, she sobbed uncontrollably. Then I confronted the demons that fed on that pain. Instantly, powerful spirits of death and abuse surfaced. The woman experienced what we call co-consciousness, meaning she was aware of all that was happening. She heard the voices of the demons and listened as they described their plans to destroy her. At that point, she'd probably have walked a tightrope across Niagara Falls if I had asked her to. It was a small thing to ask her to call on the Lord for help, asking Him to be her Savior and deliver her from Satan. She didn't hesitate for a moment, and in the process was confessing Christ as Lord and calling on His name. She was delivered that day, and felt the presence of Christ's peace in a way that Buddhism never offered. I met her at the point of her need, ministered to her shame and torment, and demonstrated the power of Christ over the devil as she'd never witnessed it with all her chants and meditation. That spoke more to her than all the sermons I could have preached about being born again.

I've followed this principle in ministering to Muslims, Sikhs, Hindus, and those of many other faiths. God is merciful, and He wants to offer the "children's bread" (Matthew 15:26) to all who are hungry. He offers water that quenches the driest soul from the wellspring of His person (John 4:13–14). I have seen that ministering deliverance without a litmus test of faith results in many coming to Christ because they experience firsthand His rescuing love. Deliverance can draw them to salvation. Dealing with demons is not only a process of spiritual liberation, it may also be a forceful tool of evangelism.

Focus on Solutions, Not Sins

The God factor can also be overplayed when the exorcism client seeking help has addictions and moral issues. What's the best way to handle an individual who is hooked on drugs or is an alcoholic? Should you refuse ministry to a sex addict until he has demonstrated that he is living a morally pure life for some designated amount of time? What if a couple who lives together seeks deliverance? Do you tell them to get married first before you'll pray for them? Do you tell a homosexual to go straight first or insist that a transgendered person stop his sex-reassignment hormone injections? I'm about to make a bold statement: if you're going to be effective in dealing with demons, don't inflict your moral agenda on others as a hurdle to receiving prayer.

I'm not suggesting that what you consider to be biblical morality is not important. What I do observe in the Gospels is that in the five main instances in which there is an anecdotal account of Christ casting out demons, there is no indication that He restricted His mercy only to those whom He considered worthy. Legion didn't have to first put on his clothes to be set free (Luke 8). He was set free and then clothed himself. The demon-possessed man in the synagogue (Mark 1) didn't have to first demonstrate his devotion to God by returning to worship for successive Sabbaths before Christ would cast out his demons. Jesus reached out to people right where they were, and He freed them to begin a new life. Too often, those ministering deliverance want to sort out all the details of propriety before they get on with the job of telling the devil where to go!

Certain Demons Have a Religious Assignment

Demons have specific assignments from Lucifer to accomplish highly complex purposes. Cracking that code I talked about earlier in the book may mean finding the agenda from hell that is driving the demonic deeds. The God-factor in this chapter means that you seek to find the spiritual intent of the demon and what religious goals he seeks to accomplish.

Once I confronted a demon who was coy about his name. "You know me, you just don't know my name," the unclean spirit teased. "You've met me lots of times; you didn't know it was me. I follow you everywhere you go; that's my assignment." I demanded, in the name of Jesus, to know what that job was. "I'm the spirit of Exorcism," he answered. "It's my assignment to discredit what you do. I tell the preachers and churches not to believe that what you do is real. I lie every way that I can to convince people that Christians can't have demons and that there's no value in the ministry of deliverance. Clever, huh?"

Keep in mind that this demon's job was very specific and also religious. Other demons may be on a mission to send chronic cases to deliverance ministers so that these well-meaning people waste a lot of time trying to help those who don't really want help. Yet other demons convince religious leaders that deliverance gets people's attention off the need for salvation, or that the command to cast out demons ended with the apostolic age. The tactics are many, but the aim is the same. Wear out or wear down deliverance ministers. Make them "grow weary in doing good" (2 Thessalonians 3:13). Get them to give up or pull back to avoid criticism or harsh judgments. Temper their approach or sequester what they do.

BACK TO DENNIS

I spent hours sorting through all the questions in the mind of Dennis. I wasn't out to respond to every issue or to settle every contradiction. I explained to him that he had a lifetime to work out what he believed about tangential beliefs of the Christian faith, doctrines that weren't rooted in salvation essentials. The time at hand would be better spent getting rid of his demons so that he could move forward with greater clarity of thought to decide what constituent aspects of faith he felt God was leading him to believe.

By interrogating Dennis's demons without the interference of his conundrums, we uncovered the real reason that religious issues were paramount in his mind. His possession was rooted in a 20-generation curse of an old Irish priest who had gotten a woman (Dennis's ancestor) pregnant and then convinced her to have an abortion to cover his tracks. She eventually married and had other children, but because she did not know how to break the sexual soul-bond with the priest, his mental and emotional agony followed through her bloodline, eventually cursing Dennis's life. That priest eventually returned to his faith and repented of his evil, but the generational backwash remained. Dennis's suppressed anger arose from a genetically inherited curse of spiritual confusion, fostered by a demon of unbelief that followed generation after generation.

Dennis's real issue wasn't how he should be baptized, whether he should pursue the spiritual gifts of First Corinthians 12, or if he should hold to a pre-, mid-, or post-trib eschatology. The demons of doubt were playing games in his mind, and by taking time to unravel his spiritual history, he was set free from evil spirits that had driven his dad to lust and tormented countless ancestors. Dennis could now set a genuinely godly example in his home and lead his children on a spiritual path that he had never walked himself.

PERSPECTIVE

Who is eligible for deliverance? This chapter makes the case that any sincerely seeking soul may be set free from demons, regardless of his or her spiritual past and current theological persuasion. However, the one barrier that seems to consistently interfere with the deliverance process is the idea that "Christians can't have demons" because "light and darkness can't dwell together." Unfortunately, these theological fallacies, which are thoroughly vetted in the courses of our International School of Exorcism, are seldom honestly addressed in any open forum of honest discussion. Consequently, the opposition sits on the sidelines spouting fallacious, worn-out arguments, when, in most cases, these detractors have never spent a single moment actually confronting an authentic case of demonic possession.

I've met and fellowshipped with hundreds of clergy and lay persons actively involved in casting out demons. Not one of them believes that being a Christian automatically exempts one from having an indwelling evil spirit. As the adage goes (reworded slightly for my application), the person who has the veracity of experience is never at the mercy of the one who has only conjectured opinion without empirical knowledge.

A lot of heat and light have been expended by opponents of the deliverance ministry when, in fact, they've never been smack-dab in the middle of a full-blown, violent demonic manifestation, charged with the responsibility of resolving the situation.

Missionaries of many theological persuasions tell me about being placed in pagan cultures and suddenly experiencing the reality of demonic activity in believers. In spite of what they encounter firsthand, they are unable to talk about it to their denominational superiors. Worse yet, they don't dare mention the subject during their time back in America while raising support for their mission.

Deliverance is one area of ministry where one's theology and personal observations must be in sync. That is why I deem it so important that, in most deliverance sessions, the one leading the ministry should seek the visual and oral manifestation of a demon. It's easier to argue that Christians don't have demons if one avoids confrontation with evil spirits who undeniably speak and act in much different ways from the host person. More important, those demons, if allowed to speak, may divulge information unknown to the host, which can later be corroborated. I've witnessed this many times, including the exposing of actual historical events, which could later be verified through research.

When a voice in an individual's body (during a demonic manifestation) speaks articulately in a language unknown to the host, something supernaturally evil is occurring and it can't be brushed off with a dismissive wave of the theological hand. I once had a public manifestation of demonic possession in one of my seminars in which a demon spoke incessantly in a tongue unknown to either me or the host. In the audience was a PhD, a university professor, who came forward to identify what was spoken as an ancient Semite language. He revealed that the demon was speaking about how he had entered the host and what his plans were for the destruction of this individual. This information led to a successful exorcism of this ancient demon.

Case closed.

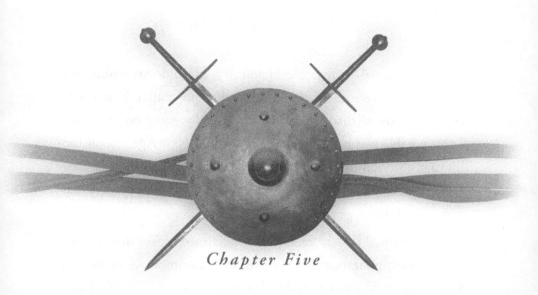

Chapter Five

WITCHCRAFT AND THE OCCULT

MARK SEEMED LIKE A NICE ENOUGH GUY. IN HIS EARLY 30S, HE WAS a rather normal-looking Bible college graduate from a very conservative, evangelical denomination. He had been raised in the church with no indication of anything unusual in his upbringing. In fact, his parents were the ones who had scheduled the Personal Spiritual Encounter with me. As he sat across from me in the conference room, I carefully studied the detailed profile we request of all our clients. I couldn't see anything unusual in his background, but once he opened his mouth and began to speak it was clear why Mom and Dad had brought him to me.

Mark's thinking was all over the place. His mind gyrated wildly from one topic to the next, sometimes making comments that were totally unrelated to my line of inquiry. He did everything possible to seize control of the conversation no matter how hard I tried to focus on discovering what was really going on in his life. Most notable was his constant babble about New Age, occult topics that obsessed him. He made disconnected references to energy fields, extraterrestrial aliens, and blue-colored auras that he saw floating around.

He explained that an older brother claimed to live in a haunted house where poltergeist phenomena were common. "I knew right away that there was a portal in his home," Mark said. "So I contacted a psychic friend to conduct a banishment ceremony. We walked through his house burning sage and chanting from the Tibetan Book of the Dead."

"Did it help?" I asked.

Mark paused. He looked perplexed. "For a while. But then the entities came back. They starting turning his TV on and off. Objects flew off shelves. I really got worried when something pushed him off a ladder, breaking his leg."

How did Mark change from being a biblically solid Bible college graduate to such an apologist for the occult? I pushed for more details.

He originally went to school to become a missionary. But he wanted to go to war-torn parts of the world, particularly the South Sudan, and no mission board would commission him. So, he signed on with a group helping to rebuild homes for poor neighborhoods in Haiti in the aftermath of the 2010 earthquake.

Shortly after that, Mark's parents noticed a gradual change in his ability to concentrate and think logically. He failed at several jobs, even though he had an advanced degree. Finally, he gave up on finding employment and came home to live with his parents. His life had been stuck since then.

THE POWER OF VOODOO

Suddenly, out of nowhere, Mark's thinking took an oblique direction. He leaned forward and spoke softly, as if letting me in on some deep secret. "They're listening to me, you know."

"They?"

"The people in the Pentagon. I write them emails and within days I see them following my policy advice. In the Middle East. Asia. Everywhere, really."

His parents looked at each other as if acknowledging that now we were getting to the real reason they brought Mark to see me.

The background information in the profile he filled out didn't indicate he'd had any psychological evaluation or intervention. I was left to make my own assessment of his mental condition.

"Mark," I said looking at him seriously, "that's not true. The Pentagon isn't taking your advice. They aren't paying any attention to your emails. They don't even know or care that you exist. It's all in your mind. You've made it up. Frankly, you talk like someone who is a paranoid schizophrenic."

He was incensed. He jerked back his head and sat up erect in a defiant pose. "Of course, you'd probably think that. You're likely in league with them."

"Them?"

"I don't have to tell you. You know who I'm talking about. The Shadow Government. The people who really call the shots. And how do I know you aren't a plant sent from them?"

I allowed him to calm down for a moment. "Mark, you're delusional. Your mind has had some kind of psychotic break with reality. What I don't know is what triggered it."

Mark's mother was in tears. She buried her face in a pile of Kleenex tissue and distressfully poured out her emotions. "He was such a good kid. He never harmed anyone. And he so wanted to be a missionary and win people to the Lord. We don't understand how it got to this...this state of...insanity."

For the moment, I didn't know either.

I asked if they knew anything about generational curses. Had they read my book on breaking curses? Was there anyone in the family who had practiced witchcraft of any kind? They were good people, but typically naïve, American evangelical Christians. They were like thousands of others I had encountered who loved the Lord but were ignorant of anything to do with spiritual warfare.

"I'm sure that there's something in the bloodline, if we go back far enough. Mark's dramatic change from Bible college student to embracing occult philosophy is too abrupt to result from any kind of natural evolution of spiritual decline. Something drastic must have occurred."

Mark sat back with an angry look on his face. He didn't like what we were saying, but it was more than that. My experiences of dealing with demons told me that there was something inside Mark that hated my assessment.

Then, instantly I had the answer, whether it was the Lord's prompting, or a bit of unconscious deduction on my part. Likely some of both. Satan's fingerprint had been right in front of me all the time, and I had missed it.

I looked past the evil glare on Mark's face, deep into his soul. "Something happened in Haiti. What was it, Mark? Did you go to any kind of Voodoo ceremony while you were there? I've been to Haiti, and you know, Mark, Voodoo and black magic witchcraft is everywhere. It's a way of life."

Mark turned serious. "Well, I didn't exactly attend any Voodoo rituals. But there was this one time..."

He cut himself off as if something inside had said, "No, don't tell."

"What happened?"

"We were helping this poor family build their home which had been destroyed. The land it had been on was too devastated with rubble to clear it, so they built the new structure a little further back in the woods, away from everything. It was on land that no one wanted, so they didn't stake an official claim of any kind. We just started laying the foundation, when one day a group of Voodoo witchdoctors stormed the area where we were. There must have been a dozen of them, all screaming in Creole. We didn't know what was going on at first, but the locals told us that the witchdoctors were angry that we were building where they held their ceremonies. They demanded that we leave immediately. But more than that..."

Mark froze with fear. His eyes grew wide and wild as if he were in terror. Haltingly, almost stuttering, he explained, "Some of them waved their hands at us in a strange way. Others got on the ground and were making strange designs with some kind of powder."

"A *veve* (vey-vey)," I explained. "A form of Voodoo demon conjuration to call up a Loa spirit."

"It was like they were cursing us somehow," Mark said, growing more agitated by the moment.

I leaned toward him and grabbed his arm to steady him. Then, I focused on his eyes which alternated from a look of madness to the cold gaze of demonic forces.

"That's when you got him, wasn't it?" I challenged the demon directly. "There must have been some preexisting curse of some kind with his ancestors."

The evil spirit shot a knowing smirk at me.

"All you needed was something in the here and now to connect to that ancestral curse. You didn't like it that Mark had a spiritual calling on his life. You had to destroy him somehow, so you waited and waited for the right moment to strike. Haiti was that moment."

The demon tried to lash out at me, but I was ready and quickly tightened my grip on Mark's arm. Now, a hideous laugh came from deep inside Mark. Then a growly voice much different from his spoke up.

"You think you're so smart, don't you?"

"No, but I do have the Holy Spirit to guide me."

"Whatever! You're right. There was a curse." The demon nodded toward the mother. "She doesn't have a clue what we did. Ask her about her grandmother who read tea leaves and told fortunes. She was really good with the pendulum and picking the sex of unborn babies."

Mom was in shock. Even though she'd brought her son for deliverance, and though she'd watched dozens of deliverances on our YouTube Exorcism Channel, witnessing an actual demonic manifestation was shocking to her mainstream Christian thinking. And this wasn't something she could sit back dispassionately and watch. This was her son!

"Whatever that thing is talking to us, it is telling the truth. My grandmother was like that. But she always said it was a gift from the Lord. We didn't know any different. Honestly, I've never heard a sermon in church, my whole life, about demons or what's wrong with that kind of activity."

After giving everyone a quick crash course in demonology 101, and explaining the dangers of any involvement with the occult, I led both parents and child in a curse-breaking prayer. Mark spoke with clarity for the first time since we had met. All of them renounced every ancestral involvement in witchcraft. Mark repeated a prayer in which I led him to cancel the curses hurled at him that day in Haiti. I also had him repent of all his personal involvement in New Age and witchcraft practices.

As we prayed, the demons grew more agitated. Mark's whole body shook as if it were being shocked by a succession of electrical jolts.

"Who are you?" I demanded.

"Witchcraft! Voodoo! Divination!" the demons screamed. "Take your pick. We're all here and we're not leaving."

"Is this man called of God to be a missionary?"

"Yes," the demon snarled.

"Now that the generational sins of the grandmother have been renounced, do you have any further legal right to Mark?"

"He called on us. He burned the sage. He contacted the psychic."

"Yes, but he asked God's forgiveness, just moments ago."

The demons were speechless. They had no comeback. It was all over; the business of casting them out was all that was left. By the authority of Christ, I forced the demons to repeat after me, a standard protocol of exorcism that I've developed over many years of experience. I'll not take space here to lay it out as it is taught in our International School of Exorcism because that information is readily available to students of the curriculum. The essence of what I demanded of the demons was to lift the Haitian curse and to declare that their rights to Mark were nullified. Then, we cast out the demons with relative ease.

When it was over, Mark's transformation was remarkable. A broad smile filled his face, and his evangelical language returned. He spoke about the Lord and His will. He spoke lovingly of his parents, and the new direction he wanted his life to take. I'm not suggesting that the exorcism solved all his problems. Several years of mental disturbances, along with demonization from his New Age obsessions, had done profound damage. It was going to take professional therapy, perhaps some medication, and the support of a church family for him to recover his nearly lost faith and mental acuity. But the curse of Haitian Voodoo was lifted, and the demons were gone. He could now genuinely heal and get back his life and the faith he had lost.

THE CURSE OF THE OCCULT

When reaching out to any individual who has dabbled in the occult, it's necessary to be as thorough as possible about renouncing their involvement in every practice of biblically forbidden witchcraft. Such occult activity may range from occasional dabbling to the habitual seeking out of psychics, daily reading of horoscopes, or participating in rituals that invoked entities, such as in a séance. The profile by which I vet Encounter clients details scores of such pitfalls. We'll not take time to list them all here. For the purposes of this book, let's consider the basic areas of danger, along with some representative examples:

Divination

Simply put, this practice is searching for what can't be determined by the natural senses. The very word "divination" is found in most Bible translations such as the Authorized King James Version (KJV) and the New International Version (NIV). See, for example, the condemnations of Deuteronomy 18:10; 2 Kings 17:17; Jeremiah 14:14; Ezekiel 12:24; 13:6, 21:23; and Acts 16:16 in the KJV. In the NIV consider Genesis 44:5, Leviticus 19:26, Deuteronomy 18:14, First Samuel 15:23, and Isaiah 2:6. Examples of divination would be horoscopes, fortune-telling, palm reading, Ouija boards, séances, reading runes, and consulting tarot cards. These examples are by no means exhaustive, but point the reader to the basic nature of divinatory devices of all kinds. Satan lures victims to attempt to pull back the veil of the unknown. The devil wants humans to dispense with trusting God for the future and instead to depend upon some occult peering into the realm of reality beyond what can be discerned by bodily senses. In the process, looking to the Lord for guidance is supplanted by leaning on human insight of some kind, accompanied by a particular device or ceremony.

Proverbs 3:5-6 admonishes us to not lean on our human understanding but, in all our ways, to acknowledge God and let Him direct our paths. Christ warned that we are to take no thought about the cares of life but to cast our cares upon the Lord, for our "heavenly Father knows that you need all these things" (Matthew 6:32). In short, if you can get specific, truthful answers about the unknown from something such as the positions of the stars and planets of the heavens, why would you ever need to call upon the Lord who created the heavens?

Prognostication

This is similar to divination, but it is specifically focused on knowing events in the chronological future by means of things such as fortune-telling. All the Scriptures and examples cited above for divination would equally apply here; specific examples of prognostication would be I Ching, crystal ball gazing, sorcery, precognition, clairvoyance, and seeking so-called "spiritual advisors" and psychics. Once again, this list is not exhaustive.

New Age Practices

Many occult endeavors could be lumped into the New Age category. Prominent in our culture for the last four decades or so, these witchcraft practices appeal to the curious and those drawn to the paranormal. They may have ancient roots but often are celebrated as pop-culture ways of rejecting traditional Christian beliefs. Included in this list would be consulting mediums/channelers, reading auras, fire-walking, parapsychology, past-life therapy, telepathy, and psychokinesis. Though originally these practices may have been tied to unsavory rituals, the New Age commonly redefines and sanitizes them for mass consumption. "Channeling," for example, is the old witchcraft art of mediumship; for New Agers it is considered a portal to the "other side," often involving contact with so-called ascended masters and spiritual "adepts" who have supposedly transcended our mundane existence.

Eastern Meditation, Mystical Traditions

The Eastern traditions of mysticism, which have been imported to the West, have opened many new doors to demonization. For the most comprehensive analysis of this danger, I refer the reader to my book *Larson's Book of World Religions*. This 575-page volume has a detailed analysis of all major Eastern mystical and meditative traditions. For our purposes here, it's important to understand the demonic dangers inherent in these disciplines that have come to our shores, mainly in variants of Buddhism, Taoism, and Hinduism. While considerable theological differences exist, mystical views of reality and spiritually have these four basic theological errors in common:

First, the idea that matter and spirit are in conflict. The material body is an enemy of the spirit and must be mortified or subjugated in some way to lessen its effect on spiritual choices. Ways of applying this principle range from the bodily positions of yoga to the ascetic practices of monks and gurus who may indulge in extreme fasts and isolation, such as not speaking or communicating for months and even years. The idea is to still or even to kill the senses so that "pure" spirit may emerge in its quest for self-realization. The spiritual consequence is supposed to be the "enlightened" conclusion that one's individual ego is divine, the god-within; there is no external, transcendent deity to which one may be morally accountable. This idea of self-deification harkens back to the serpent's lie in Eden, found in Genesis 3:5: "Your eyes will be opened, and you will be like God." This is the ultimate blasphemy and it opens the door to the evil, lying Anti-Christ spirits of Blasphemy and Deception.

Second, the concept that sin is non-existent as an objective moral reality. Swami Vivekananda's Self-Realization Fellowship for many years ran ads in major publications declaring, "It is a sin to say that there is sin." Clever. If there is no definable evil, but merely one's alienation from the understanding that the self is god, then right and wrong must be decided by each individual's internal and relative moral compass. Students of Eastern mysticism who believe this lie are unable to receive freedom from demons.

All deliverance from Satan is a quest for truth, which John 8:32 tells us makes us free. Deliverance from demonic bondage requires changing a person's moral behavior, but an individual who negates the very idea of definable sin is left incapable of deciding what sins to cease in order to pull down a particular demonic stronghold. In my experience of thousands of cases of deliverance, those who have studied or practiced Eastern religions have a significant moral barrier to get past. They must renounce the idea that sin is merely a lack of intuitively connecting with some inner energy (which eradicates the need for repentance). They must turn from the lie that the self is god.

Third, the notion that meditative practices are the means of achieving a spiritually enlightened state of being. Almost all Eastern meditation, from Zen to Transcendental Meditation, is based on this concept: mind is the enemy of spirit, and by emptying the mind the meditator descends to deeper levels of understanding the oneness of all existence. The mind must be quieted, even destroyed, because it is believed to be the center of all false desires. Indeed, classical Buddhism teaches that evil comes, not from actions, but from desires of the senses. Kill the senses and you kill the desire.

This withdrawal, even to the point of trances and catatonic states, is clearly an opening for demonic invasion. In effect, the will is silenced or neutralized and thus offers no resistance, especially in deep meditation, to any demonic incursions. In fact, some meditation disciplines teach that the entry of entities during deep, seated meditation is to be welcomed. I've often encountered demonized former meditators who trance-out during times of Christian prayer. These spirits of mind-control are so strong that they can almost instantly induce a detached state of blanked consciousness, which prohibits the seeker from praying or renouncing these practices.

Fourth, the conviction that the guru is the gateway to god. Powerful soul ties are formed with the spiritual teacher whom the client for deliverance may have followed in the past. They were likely taught, in a tradition rooted in Hinduism, that the way to god is through a guru. (Think for a moment how far our culture has spiritually declined; a few decades ago the average American had never heard the word "guru.") Often, such as in Transcendental Meditation, the neophyte meditator is encouraged to bring fruit and flower offerings to the guru, even to prostate himself before this religious figure. This means that the meditator may have idolatrously given offerings to the teacher of the current guru and also to that teacher's teacher, and so on back any number of generations; thus, a demonic multigenerational soul-bond has been created which must be renounced in detail.

False Prophets

If there is any indication that the seeker of deliverance has been involved in any kind of cultic teaching, two things must be repudiated. First, the teachings of any and all biblically aberrational systems of belief must be renounced. Second, the leader, prophet, or founder of the false religious cult must also be disowned. When breaking the bondage of the teaching, there may be resistance from a demon whose assignment is to keep the client in submission to the cult's ideas. Be persistent to root out all teachings that may be residually adhered to even after leaving the cult. And be specific. While it's not necessary to renounce every single element of ideology, the most significant false doctrines must be placed under the blood of Christ. Examples would be the ascendency to godhood in Mormonism or the belief that Jesus Christ was actually the archangel Michael in Jehovah's Witnesses.

Regarding the renouncing of all allegiance to the false prophet(s) of the cult, there may be a strong soul tie that developed during the time in the cult. Using Mormonism as an example again, adherents of the Church of Jesus Christ of Latter Day Saints are taught that they may attest to the authenticity of their founder, Joseph Smith Jr., by declaring a "burning in their bosom." Whatever that may mean existentially, it is a powerful soul tie between the spiritual forces that compelled Smith and that now torment the exiting cult member. Other examples might include Maharishi Mahesh Yogi of Transcendental Meditation, the guru Sai Baba, Charles Taze Russell of the Watchtower Society (or any Kingdom Hall leader of Jehovah's Witnesses), the Buddha of Buddhism, Mohammed of Islam, or Reverend Moon of the Unification Church. I have chosen well-known examples, but the person receiving ministry may have belonged to less easily identifiable, more clandestine groups. The size and influence of the group in question doesn't matter. What's important is the bond formed by involvement in the cult and adherence to its ideology. In some cases, what I call a Dissociated Soul Transference (explained in detail in our International School of Exorcism) may occur. In this case, the deliverance minister might actually speak to an embedded soul-identity of the cult leader. That dissociated identity must be told to leave and the demon attached to it expelled.

Demonic Documents

Every codified writing or communication from false religious systems must be renounced and such documents destroyed. I often discover that even when people sincerely seek deliverance they may be still mentally bound by spirits of mind control because they keep in their possession such volumes as *The Teachings of Buddha* (Buddhism), the *Tibetan Book of the Dead* (Tibetan Buddhism), the *Book of Mormon* (Mormonism), the *Bhagavad Gita* (Hinduism), the *New World Translation Bible* (Jehovah's Witnesses), *The Satanic Bible*, or *A Course in Miracles.* Because these writings have been a past source of indoctrination, the deceiving spirits fomenting these beliefs may use the actual book as a point of spiritual contact. (In our cyber age, writings based on false doctrines also need to be erased from the computer and all computing devices.)

PERSPECTIVE

All that I have detailed above is but a very small portion of occult teachings and belief systems that must be removed from the life of someone who is seeking deliverance. Our Personal Spiritual Encounter Profile lists more than 100 examples to be considered, and there are many hundreds more that, except for practical brevity, might have been included. Because Satan's ingenuity to deceive is complex beyond human ken, great care must be taken to be as thorough as possible with occult renunciations. Although it is impossible and impractical to address every occult entanglement in the life of a person—I often meet people who have spent upwards of 10, 20, even more than 30 years involved in various forms of witchcraft—ask the Holy Spirit to direct attention to the most salient and corrosive beliefs and concentrate on the demons attached to these false doctrines. Then, while the deliverance minister may not be able to probe every entanglement, the most important strongholds can be pulled down to bring spiritual relief and a cleansing of the mind from all spirits operating through "doctrines of demons" (1 Timothy 4:1).

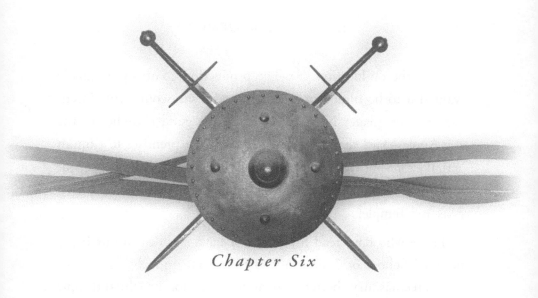

Chapter Six

SLEUTHING SPIRITS
OF BODY AND SOUL

SEVERAL YEARS AGO I FILMED A TELEVISION REALITY SHOW CALLED *The Real Exorcist*. It consisted of 16 one-half-hour episodes which could be aired independently or combined for eight one-hour shows. It originally aired in England, then South Korea (where it was the number one show for several months), and after that in various international markets, eventually ending up on the U.S. channel SyFy. Each of the 16 episodes featured a different exorcism in a different city in America and England. One of the shows was filmed in New York City, and it's that episode which included an encounter unique in all my years of ministering deliverance. What made it so unusual?

First, the on-location site. The production company originally wanted it to be filmed in a church, and a site-scout went searching all over greater New York. When the good churches of the Big Apple heard that we wanted to use their premises to film an actual exorcism, they all turned us down. Several days were spent looking for a suitable site, and only one consented: the Brooklyn Masonic Temple!

Those who have read my books or have enrolled in our International School of Exorcism know what an unlikely choice this was. Freemasonry, better known to some for its philanthropic work through organizations such as Shriner's hospitals, is a shadowy and sometimes downright demonic organization that behind closed doors conducts secret, occult ceremonies which are off-limits to outsiders.

I'll not take time here to cite all the dangers of Freemasonry. In brief summary, various degrees of the Masons require the reciting of blood oaths that subject the neophyte to deadly consequences should he ever reveal what goes on behind closed doors. If a Mason ever tells anyone, even a spouse or family member, what happens in the clandestine ceremonies, that lodge member has bound himself by vows, reinforced by oaths, swearing that he will have his throat slit, his tongue ripped out, and his innards disemboweled. And that's just for starters in the early stages of ascension through multiple "degrees" in the Masonic lodge.

I have exposed such evil elements of Freemasonry for many years and earned the ire of thousands of deceived Masons. I have also performed hundreds of exorcisms on individuals who became demon-possessed because either they or their forebears were Masons. Rising through the degrees of the lodge is a dangerous spiritual journey that few fully comprehend until it is too late. It's true that many lodges are just "good ol' boy" clubs where success in the local community depends on having a network of fellow Masons. And some lodges, especially in America's Bible Belt, have a vaguely Christian emphasis in their ritual.

But here is what makes the Freemasons so dangerous. Because the rituals and ceremonies are hidden, and because all members are bound by a verbalized death curse should they disclose what goes on, such secrecy is open to exploitation by nefarious individuals. And because the history of Freemasonry is steeped in the worship of Lucifer and the goings-on inside the lodge are covered by a cloak of mutually pledged concealment, diabolical things have occurred. My files contain many case studies of exorcisms performed on individuals who claimed to be victims of Freemason ritual sex abuse and even extortion and murder. Their possessing demons confirmed the accusations. (I once met a Shriner attending a convention in the same hotel where I was holding a seminar; he proudly wore a Mason's fez with the crescent of Islam on it and a jacket with signage on the back declaring his allegiance to the Jezebel Lodge!)

Yet, here I was walking boldly where no exorcist had gone before: through the massive 20-foot front doors of the Brooklyn Masonic Lodge. What I saw next was stunning. Hanging from the ceiling just inside the entry were two signs. One was a banner misquoting Scripture: "With Hope All Things Are Possible." (It should have read: "With *God* all things are possible"—Matthew 19:26). The second sign was a pentagram. Not a pentacle, as is found in witchcraft, with the single point of a five-pointed star extended upward but rather a pentagram, on which two of the five points reach upward, and the single point aims downward. (It's believed that the pentagram is the classic image of Lucifer—goatee pointing downward and the two points protruding vertically as the two points of Lucifer's Baphomet goat-image horns.)

"Wow," I thought to myself, "not much doubt there about what's really behind the lodge."

IN THE SEAT OF THE WORSHIPFUL MASTER

With the camera crew we climbed several flights of stairs to a large room where various kinds of meetings were held, and where the exorcism would be filmed. As the crew began setting cameras and lights, which for a network show can take an inordinate amount of time, I wandered around. A Christian friend had joined me for the TV shoot. In minutes we found ourselves facing the door to the main ceremonial hall. There wasn't any "No Entry" sign, so we walked inside.

The room was massive, big enough to hold a tennis tournament. I estimated that the ceiling was more than 30 feet high. Near the top there were frescos and bas-relief images incorporating the symbols of major world religions. Because they were so near the ceiling they appeared small, but I calculated the images were about six to eight feet in height. One pagan religion after another was celebrated in art, including the Babylonians, Assyrians, Egyptians, Greeks, and Romans. Each tribute featured the relevant gods and goddesses. Notably missing? Not a single Christian symbol. Not one cross in the whole place.

There was no question which spiritual forces were being commemorated; all the tributes were to demonic systems of belief. Knowing I was about to film an exorcism in these evil surroundings, my friend and I decided to pray-walk around the room several times, invoking the blood of Christ. We stopped at the front of the huge hall. Though we had never been in an actual

Masonic lodge inner sanctum before, there was no mistaking the massive chair resting on a large dais. This was the seat of the lodge's leader, the so-called Worshipful Master. Above the chair was the occult-themed square and compass of Freemasonry. This was where men had been seated for the dark ceremonies when entrants to the lodge were forced to wear a hood over their heads ("hoodwinked"), being led to this spot with a long rope about their neck (a "cable-tow"). It was here that, in many lodges, they might hold a Koran in their hands, in tribute to the Islamic dedications of the Shriners. And in not a few lodges they would drink wine or even blood from a human skull.

As a reader, you may have raised your eyebrows by this point. How could this be? You know Masons, even Shriners. You have some in your family. You can't imagine Dad or Grandpa doing such things. So, go ahead and ask them. Here is the challenge; they are bound by a blood oath to refuse to answer or to lie.

As I stood before the Worshipful Master's chair, I couldn't resist the urge to sit down where no exorcist had ever sat before—in the seat of Lucifer. Just my friend and I were in the room, so I stood on the arm of the chair, and with anointing oil, reached up to place the sign of the cross right on the symbol of Luciferianism. I then sat in the chair and claimed the blood of Christ over any future proceedings to take place in this citadel of Satan.

I should interject that a 19th-century man named Albert Pike is considered to be the American father of Freemasonry, particularly in the Southern Jurisdiction of the Lodge. He wrote an influential Freemason book entitled *Morals and Dogma*. Among the statements attributed to him is this:

That which we must say to the world is that we worship a god, but it is the god that one adores without super-stition. To you, Sovereign Grand Inspectors General, we say this, that you may repeat it to the brethren of the 32nd, 31st and 30th degrees: The masonic Religion should be, by all of us initiates of the higher degrees, maintained in the Purity of the Luciferian doctrine. If Lucifer were not God, would Adonay and his priests calumniate him? Yes, Lucifer is God.

There is some dispute about the exact source of this quote, which may or may not have originated with Pike; however, note that Pike also declared, "Lucifer, the Light-bearer! Strange and mysterious name to give to the Spirit of Darkness! Lucifer, the Son of the Morning! Is it he who bears the Light, and with its splen-dors intolerable, blinds feeble, sensual, or selfish souls? Doubt it not!" (Just try to figure out this antiquated mode of expression!)

Masons have twisted logic and Christian teaching to try and explain away Pike's bold proclamations of Satanism, which are a constant theme of his writings. They also deny the author-ity of Scripture, some even claiming that the fall of Lucifer was a Christian invention to demean the supposed "true" intentions of Lucifer.

Volumes of assenting and dissenting opinions have been writ-ten as to the authenticity of the above quotes and other of Pike's endorsements of demonism. But to those who read *Morals and Dogma,* it is clear that Pike was a powerful occultist who indulged various forms of paganism, mythology, and witchcraft, incor-porating them into the teachings of the lodges over which he had sway.

In *Morals and Dogma,* Pike blasphemously gave Freemasons his own "Ten Commandments," corrupting the actual Decalogue and attributing his teaching to "God...Immutable Wisdom and Supreme Intelligence." He even proudly declared that "Masonry is identical with the ancient Mysteries."

There are scores of Internet sites which argue the pros and cons of Masonry's attachment to the demonic. I can attest that I have read *Morals and Dogma,* and the above quotes are mild compared to the true intentions of Freemasonry as stated in that book. Only brevity prevents me from including other outrageous claims of Pike. I also have hundreds of documented exorcisms involving the demon Lucifer possessing the souls of former Freemasons, and, in some cases, those whose ancestors belonged to the Lodge. For more exhaustive information, read the Freemasonry section of my book *Larson's Book of World Religions.*

A Man Named Malcolm

So much for Albert Pike and the demonic influences in Freemasonry. Back to the Brooklyn temple where I was to film.

My goal accomplished in this unholy of unholies, my friend and I returned to the room where the exorcism would occur. Lights were set. Cameras were ready. A 20-something young man named Malcolm walked into the room and sat down in front of me, where the director had positioned him. Blocking out any distractions from the filming crew, I proceeded to quiz him in the manner that I teach in this book.

I quickly learned that Malcolm had been a longtime student of all forms of the occult. He rattled off one demonic indulgence after another, almost totally unaware of the dark dangers of what he had been investigating. So, why was he there? He explained that the deeper he went into these realms, the more he began to suffer mentally and physically. His body suffered unusual pains for which the doctors could find no cause or cure. Depression began to take over. He felt as though his thoughts weren't his own. Voices filled his head. They talked to him and they talked to each other, mostly about spiritual topics. Gradually, these voices began suggesting that Malcolm was a worthless human being who deserved to die. Better yet, he should do the world a favor and end his own life.

As we talked his mind gyrated wildly, at times to the point of near incoherency. He rambled about aliens and superhumans, about government conspiracies and telepathic communication from celestial beings. Clearly, he did have demons, but he was also suffering from some mental condition that couldn't be diagnosed or resolved in this setting. He definitely was paranoid.

I struggled to reason with him, but no matter what I said the voices contradicted me. "There are demons inside you," I explained. "You've opened the door by all the occult stuff you've done. Only turning to Christ and receiving an exorcism will ultimately cure you. Plus, you need some serious professional therapeutic intervention and medication."

Suddenly he lunged at me. My friend, who until then had been just off-camera, quickly jumped in front of the camera to grab Malcolm. A violent physical struggle ensued. I pleaded with Malcolm to renounce all his witchcraft. He did so, though it seemed at the time more out of sheer terror at what was happening rather than an admission of spiritual fault. Still, I went on with the exorcism until Malcolm collapsed, writhing on the floor. After a hideous scream that echoed throughout the cavernous lodge, he fell silent.

I knelt by his side, anointed him with oil to fill the spiritual vacancy in his soul left by the departing demons, and helped him to his feet. The TV crew was on a tight schedule to get on to the next episode location, so I quickly instructed Malcolm on some basic spiritual principles. I strongly encouraged him to seek the help and advice of mental health professionals to deal with his delusions. I have no idea whether or not he did. Which brings me to the second reason this exorcism was unique.

About six months later, after all the editing work on *The Real Exorcist* had been completed and this episode was ready to air, I got a call from the production company. They wanted me to get on a plane as soon as possible and come to California and film another episode to replace the one filmed with Malcolm. Malcolm had committed suicide a few days earlier and his parents requested that this episode not air. We, of course, agreed.

Out of nearly 40,000 documented case studies of exorcisms spanning four decades, this is only one of three times that I know of when someone to whom I've directly ministered later killed themselves because of mental health issues they refused to address. While that is a noteworthy statistic, it is three too many. Malcolm's sad death spurred me to increase my efforts to understand better the issues surrounding mental illness and the demonic link connecting spirits of infirmity to specific diseases. That is why in the International School of Exorcism we teach several courses on basic approaches to human psychology and the most common forms of mental illness that a deliverance minister might encounter.

We have no intention to claim that our students are mental health care professionals nor are they prepared to clinically diagnose an individual's state of mind; however, we face a stark reality.

Clergy and lay ministers often encounter those whose minds and bodies are wracked by both demonic forces as well as neurological and biochemical stresses. Even a cursory layman's understanding of these matters can help those called to minister to more effectively direct their clients toward proper medical and psychological solutions when necessary.

I am saddened to this day at the loss of Malcolm's life and the pain it caused those who loved him. I honestly believe that, given the context of our encounter, I did all that I could for him at the time. Unfortunately, it appears that the mental illness he suffered either took its own toll or was manipulated by whatever demons we couldn't expel at the time due to his incomplete cooperation.

To help you, the reader, better understand this battle for the body, mind, and soul of those who seek spiritual guidance (see 1 Thessalonians 5:23), let's look at some of the factors that may be encountered within the context of an individual seeking deliverance for demonic oppression.

THE MIND/BODY CONNECTION

Many Eastern religions, New Age advocates, and modern psychiatry share a common viewpoint. It is sometimes referred to as the "mind/body connection." This is how some health care professionals combine metaphysical spiritual concepts with traditional secular modalities in medicine. There is, of course, an element of truth in this. Emotions obviously affect the way we feel mentally and physically. Unwelcome intrusions in our lives such as the loss of a job, death of a loved one, illness or injury, and financial difficulties profoundly affect our mental and physical health. That is obvious. Stress and depression speak back to us through our bodies. When something is out of equilibrium, it takes a toll on how we feel and think.

Doctors recognize that any number of physical symptoms may have origins in the mind. These maladies may include chest pain, fatigue, aches, headaches, high blood pressure, palpitations of the heart, sexual dysfunction, stomach disorders, and weight gain or loss. The immune system may be compromised, leading to infections and susceptibility to everything from colds to major diseases. Most people go to a doctor to identify the source of pain in the body. But a good physician will also ask the right questions to understand what may be the root of the matter, instead of just prescribing a pill for the symptoms.

A deliverance minister, to be effective, needs to be a kind of spiritual doctor and have a holistic approach to combatting the work of Satan. Getting an individual free from demonic attack is about more than screaming commands at demons or jumping into the fray of spiritual warfare. An effective exorcism is one in which all aspects of a person's behavior and psychosomatic conditions are considered, especially when it's apparent that all is not well physically and emotionally.

To demonstrate how powerful this connection of mind and body can be, let's look at the developing science of psychoneuroimmunology. Recent research at the University of Virginia has discovered a direct link between the brain and the immune system, via lymphatic vessels. This connection was not previously known to exist. Lymphatic vessels are similar to blood vessels, which carry blood throughout the body. Lymphatic vessels carry immune cells throughout the body; however, it was long believed that such vessels stopped before reaching the brain. Now, that assumption is being questioned. Doctors conducting this research believe that this discovery could be used to better understand and treat diseases such as autism, multiple sclerosis, and Alzheimer's. What now seems to be clear is that the brain, the immune system, *and* gut microbes are intricately linked.[1] Truly, as human beings we are "fearfully and wonderfully made" (Psalm 139:14).

Here is the essence of these new discoveries. There may be an identifiable direct pathway from the gut to the brain, and vice versa. In addition to the nervous system of the brain, the gut is embedded with an enteric nervous system which works both independently of and in conjunction with the brain. Communication between the brain in the skull and the gut nervous system channels in both directions. That is why stress and anxiety make the stomach sick. Ever felt butterflies in your stomach? Well, that's what this is all about.

This bidirectional system makes it possible for the brain to affect one's susceptibility to disease by how it feels and what it thinks; similarly, what's going on in the gut-brain, the "enteric nervous system," may profoundly affect the emotions and influence factors such as depression, moods, and mental disorders. Simply put, an unhealthy body means an unhealthy mind and the possibility of brain disorders and vice versa.

Although psychiatrists and neuroscientists are now figuring this out, Satan has certainly known about this for a long time. This information sheds neurological and biochemical light on biblical truths such as these:

> *A merry heart makes a cheerful countenance, but by sorrow of the heart the spirit is broken* (Proverbs 15:13).

A merry heart does good, like medicine, but a broken spirit dries the bones (Proverbs 17:22).

For as he thinks in his heart, so is he (Proverbs 23:7).

To understand the import of these verses, use "heart" and "mind" interchangeably. Do you get the picture, from a neurological and brain-enteric system perspective?

What does this all mean to the one who deals with the devil? In many cases a deliverance minister has to consider the physical condition and the state of mental health of the client. Don't misunderstand. We're not assuming that an exorcist or prayer minister has either the necessary medical or psychological training to support a comprehensive view of a client's mental and physical state. But from at least a peripheral perspective, the total mind-body state of the client must often be analyzed before embarking on an exorcism.

The Systemic Bond of the Body to the Demonic

Those who aren't familiar with our modality of deliverance may find it strange that I'm concerned about knowing an individual's state of mind and health. From what the reader has already learned in this chapter, my purposes should be evident. As stated earlier, I'm not making either medical or psychological diagnoses. But I am trying to get a sense of the whole person and how evil spirits may have attacked in more than obvious ways. Let's consider the area of physical health.

First, a warning. There are some deliverance ministers who make almost ironclad declarations about the correlation between diseases and their emotional roots. I believe that is ill-advised. I appreciate the contribution to understanding this mind/body matter that such individuals have made. However, there is danger when, lacking true medical training, anyone makes claims that certain soul issues will almost always result in a particular disease. Such deterministic cause-effect predictions may disregard any number of biochemical and neurological factors. It may also lead the suffering person to forego proper allopathic treatment, which can be injurious, even life-threatening. It may not be wise to avoid proper medical intervention such as chemotherapy or surgery because an individual concludes that the problem exists only in his emotions. While it's true in some instances that healing the mind also heals the body, this determination should not be reached without wise medical consultation.

Now, having advised prudence and caution regarding health issues, here are some of the things that I do look for when considering the demonic link to the body and mind.

Based on my experiences, some illness and infirmities tend to have more demonic involvement, such as fibromyalgia, certain skin conditions, intestinal disorders, cancers, and blood diseases. The presence of a disease doesn't always mean that one has a demon. But if there is a long history of family tendencies toward certain maladies, it may indicate a particular curse to which evil spirits have been attached. As indicated earlier, comprehensive curse-breaking should be considered as a spiritual countermeasure to confronting infirmities. Upon rigorous interrogation during exorcisms, some demons have revealed to me that ancient blood ceremonies/covenants have brought specific health issues into the family bloodline. I've actually had demons refer to everything from asthma to autism, declaring, "Her/his ancestors sacrificed to Moloch, and that gave us the right to physically attack in this way."

When suffering a physical disorder for which there seems to be no medical diagnosis or cure, it's important to offer a prayer such as, "Lord, whatever evil my ancestors committed that may have brought this disease on my body, I place that evil under the blood of Christ. I cancel any and all contracts or assignments on my health and receive the healing of Christ for this particular infirmity." Reminder, my book *Curse Breaking* has scores of prayers, some for particular health problems; these intercessions are in print and ready for the reader to apply.

Lessons from a Daughter of Abraham

The Bible contains the account of Christ healing the demon-possessed woman whom Jesus referred to as a "daughter of Abraham," a devout woman of faith (Luke 13). The Lord specifically declared that Satan had bound the woman. She had been this way for 18 years: bent over and unable to straighten her body. We learn from Scripture that she appeared to be suffering from some musculoskeletal disorder or rheumatoid arthritis. Perhaps she had degenerative spinal deterioration or had suffered an injury affecting discs in her back. Whatever had happened physically, it was an open door to demons.

Our International School of Exorcism training has a comprehensive and detailed analysis of this scriptural account which is very revealing and should be consulted. For our purposes in this book, note that the disease afflicting this woman had come upon her at a particular time 18 years prior. Christ is emphasizing that her physical condition was the result of a particular event, and that she became susceptible to demonic invasion at a particular point in time. She had not always been thus afflicted by either the disease or the demons. Thus, it seems likely that her physical state was the result of some emotionally traumatic occurrence which allowed this infirmity-causing evil spirit to enter.

Had she been raped as an adult or molested as a child? Did she suffer domestic violence? Did someone who hated her, for whatever reason, do some witchcraft to curse her? My spiritual hunch is that whatever happened deeply injured this woman's mind/soul, and that event opened the door for Satan to attack her body. Speculation regarding possible causes could be endless. The important point is that some emotional event of 18 years earlier had opened a demonic door resulting in deformity of the body.

Here Christ clearly demonstrates that what we suffer in the mind can result in physical ailments and that, furthermore, deliverance may be the key to physical healing. In the Gospels there are others whom Christ healed *without* casting out demons. In the case of this woman, Jesus healed by exorcism. This fact should not be lost on those Christians who have spiritual gifts of healing but who have eschewed the deliverance ministry. The lesson here is that, if there is any reasonable suspicion the root cause of the disease is demonic in nature, physical healing by the anointing and the laying on of hands should often be accompanied by prayers of deliverance.

CONFRONTING MENTAL ILLNESSES ROOTED IN THE DEMONIC

I dedicate this section of the book to the memory of Malcolm mentioned earlier in this chapter. Let me reiterate. I did counsel him to seek further mental health treatment. I did recommend that he likely needed medication to stabilize his delusions. I left it to him and his family to proceed further with proper medical treatment following our first deliverance encounter; however, since he failed to do that, there was little more that I could have done to prevent his tragedy. It's in the hope of preventing other such calamities that I offer the following thoughts.

Once again I defer to the thorough training in our School of Exorcism. Much that the reader needs to know about mental health and demons is contained in that teaching. I strongly encourage those who minister deliverance to have at least a general knowledge of the kinds of mental health issues which may be encountered in ministry, to know the clues to spotting the symptoms. Mental maladies may include schizophrenia, bipolar disorder, psychosis, borderline personality disorder, dissociative identity disorder (DID), clinical depression, obsessive compulsive spectrum disorders (OCD), and post-traumatic stress disorder (PTSD), to name a few.

The most important question for the Christian counselor or deliverance minister is whether or not demons are involved, either as a root cause or in the role of demonic exploitation. There are no indisputable diagnostic guidelines which will always resolve this dilemma; however, let me offer a few insights to guide the process of determining when or if to engage demonic forces when there seems to be some form of mental disturbance:

- If clients are currently regularly seeing mental health professionals, be cautious about aggressively praying for them. You don't want to do something that might mentally destabilize them. You also want to avoid possible ethical violations regarding interference with treatment in progress.

- The client may need to be medicated before any effective prayer ministry can occur. Delusional thoughts or erratic behavior may make it impossible to rationally deal with the crucial issues such as forgiveness, repentance, and renunciations. Certain anxiety issues may make behavior too erratic for prayer intervention. The minister/counselor also wants to avoid the possibility of the client having some kind of psychotic break which could raise serious ethical issues.

- If the client is already medicated you may not be able to effectively confront/interrogate the demons until the prescribed dosages have been cut back. I have often suggested that people seeking help go to their doctors and, if possible, engage in a process of gradually diminishing medications. Demons are emotional beings and operate through the emotional capacities of the host. If the host is heavily sedated, critical information that needs to be derived from the demons may not be accessible.

- Approach suicidal ideation with much caution. If life-threatening impulses or actual attempts have been part of a client's past, he or she should be warned to seek professional help immediately. Unfortunately, as with Malcolm, clients may not always make the minister/counselor aware of the severity their self-destructive compulsions.

- Integrating healing prayers and actual exorcism into the ministry of deliverance for the mentally challenged is often a painstaking, gradual process. Never move too quickly in this aspect of ministry. The destabilized mind takes time to recover and patience is necessary, especially when there have been delusions.

- When attempting to help an individual whose thinking is out of touch with reality, a full commitment to truth is always necessary. If it is truth which "makes us free" (see John 8:32), the minister must not shy away from kindly insisting that the mentally ill person adhere to behavior and thinking which can lead to their healing.

- When dangerous, even violent, behavior is a risk, public and private safety must be the foremost consideration, and a strictly spiritual approach to mental health problems is insufficient. In recent years there have been a tragic number of mass shootings. Many such crimes have been committed by individuals who had Christian upbringings and even made public professions of faith. Steven Jones, the shooter at the University of Northern Arizona on October 9, 2015, was a Christian homeschooled youth. I have no inside knowledge about what went wrong; however, I do know that there must have been warning signs of which family and friends were not aware.

I also know of quite a few cases in which mentally disturbed Christians have committed suicide. My point is that apparent faith in Christ is no assurance that such an individual, if psychologically unsound, will be prevented by his or her faith from engaging in injurious behavior. Their deeds may be driven by mental illness and/or demonization. What's important is getting these potentially dangerous people help and taking their threats and mental disturbances seriously.

THE MIND OR THE DEVIL? SOME CASE STUDIES

Experience is the best teacher, and I want to share with you some of what I have learned firsthand.

When to Call 911

I once received an emergency call from people whom I knew who had sat under my ministry. They asked me urgently to come to their home and help their daughter. When I arrived, the distressed mother and father led me to the living room where their young daughter, stark naked, was pacing the floor mumbling about a sexual relationship she was having with a famous public figure, someone she had never met. The parents also revealed that, just prior to my arrival, this woman had gone to the kitchen, taken a large carving knife from a drawer, and threatened to kill them. They insisted that I immediately intervene and cast out their daughter's demons.

Though I did say a brief prayer, I counseled that they should call 911 immediately and ask for a psychiatric intervention team to come as soon as possible. The parents were incensed that I didn't do an exorcism to solve the problem. They just couldn't understand that the crisis of a young woman having a psychotic break and threatening to kill would not be solved by instant deliverance. I told them that I did have Christ's authority to confront a demon manifestation, but I did not have spiritual jurisdiction over a mentally deranged mind that was menacing others with intent to do bodily harm.

Eventually, the ambulance arrived and the woman was put in a straitjacket and taken to the psychiatric ward. Sadly, the parents were so angry at me for not curing the problem on the spot that they never spoke to me again.

In the area of mental health there is a time for spiritual confrontation and there is also a time for practical intervention. The wise deliverance minister will discern the difference.

The Danger of Enabling Delusional Behavior

I was once asked to do an exorcism on a 20-something man whom the mother described as having been a popular student and athlete but who now suffered from a personality disorder. When I entered the house, I encountered the following scene. The young man, John, was lying on the couch naked but covered by a wool blanket. He was watching a soap opera on TV and eating junk snacks while guzzling one bottle of Coke after another. In fact, there were multiple cases of Coca-Cola sitting in the room. This was all that he ate! I was told that this normal young man had suddenly snapped about a year earlier and had ever since been lying on the couch. He got up only to relieve himself. In that year he had not shaved or taken a bath. The stench was unbearable.

I first asked if there were any guns in the house (there were), and insisted that they had to be put outside before I'd do anything. I then demanded that the television be shut off and told John to sit upright and face me. The mother was expecting me to start anointing him with oil and wielding my cross and Bible. Instead, I told John that I wouldn't do anything until he first got off that couch, shaved, and bathed. He protested vigorously with wildly irrational comments. I stood my ground until he angrily walked to the bathroom. Moments later we heard the water of the shower running. In about ten minutes John emerged, clean shaven and smelling considerably better.

Then, I said deliverance prayers for him. The mother was amazed at the dramatic change that had occurred so suddenly. In reality, I had no "magic bullet." I just required that, in order for spiritual help to be applied, John first had to be committed to truth—in this case, the truth that his mental problems had been accommodated for and enabled by his mother. He was a filthy mess, eating and drinking his way toward a complete physical breakdown to accompany his psychotic behavior. For me to effectively pray for him, he had to first accept the truth that his irrational thinking was being coddled out of fear and that he had to make some changes in his status, changes which he was capable of effecting.

Granted, there are some mentally ill people who are so far gone that they require institutionalization for their own safety and the safety of others. Short of that, cases such as this one can be helped with intervention that requires a yielding to the truth of the circumstances; there must be cooperation to change the situation to a more healthy status. The last I heard, this man was making considerable progress toward sounder mental health and had stopped his marathon junk food binges. He was clothed and in more of a right mind. Why? Because my deliverance modality insisted that everyone in the family remain committed to truth and not be sucked into the communal sickness of denying an intolerable environment.

The Folly of Ignoring the Potential for Violent Behavior

In the instance of yet another "house call," the family of a disturbed man sought my services as an exorcist to help their middle-aged child, named Jared. He still lived at home and remained, most of the time, sequestered in his bedroom. The family cared for him, even taking food to his room because he seldom left. The absurdity of the situation was such that the parents wanted deliverance prayers even though Jared was not physically present in the living room where we were meeting. Somehow I was expected to cast out Jared's presumed demons while he, being totally uncooperative, was in his bedroom with the door locked. The desperation of the family was such that they themselves had emotionally bought into a collective emotional sickness that denied reality.

After talking with the parents about their son for several hours, Jared abruptly appeared to join our conversation. He ranted illogically about how the world was out to get him. When I asked about any social activities that he engaged in, he became agitated and insisted that no one could be trusted as a friend. All he needed was for his parents to buy him a car and everything would be fine. I challenged him to get a job and help support the family. He became enraged, insisting that there were no good jobs to be had, and, anyway, people were too prejudiced because of his Middle Eastern identity to hire him. Then, Jared stormed out of the house in a fit of rage.

Before leaving, I asked to see Jared's bedroom hoping to find some clues to his mental behavior in there. As we stepped inside the door, I observed a large, tall safe, the kind used to store weapons. The parents told me that Jared kept more than a dozen rifles locked inside. They admitted that he wasn't a hunter, they had never known him to fire them, and he seemed to have no rational motive to keep such an arsenal. The reader can readily understand why I was concerned. I told the parents that they had to report this matter to the authorities, and that I didn't want to read in the newspapers about their son being the next mass killer. The parents shrugged off my comments and instead turned on me. They were upset about having made a donation to our ministry to cover the considerable travel costs of flying to their city. They faulted me for not being willing or able to cast out Jared's demons.

More times than I care to acknowledge, I have seen such denial regarding a troubled person's mental condition. Of all people, I recognize what demons can do, especially with someone who is emotionally unstable. But practical precautions must never be set aside when an individual's mind may be so disturbed that a deliverance-only approach may have potentially disastrous consequences.

A Plea for Cooperation

One of the things I find most grievous about the parallel realities of mental illness and demonization is the lack of understanding, communication, and cooperation between many deliverance ministers and the therapeutic community. Some clinicians take such a secular approach that they ignore, or worse yet mock, any talk of a spiritual approach to healing disturbed minds. Likewise, too many in deliverance ministries make no effort to understand the psychological viewpoint of human behavior, considering all such talk to be "of the devil."

Sadly, the majority who claim to cast out demons don't even know that the *Diagnostic and Statistical Manual of Mental Disorders*, the standard classification of mental disorders used by psychiatrists and mental health professionals, even exists. I've met deliverance ministers who claim to be "experts" who don't know the difference between a psychologist and a psychiatrist, and if the state in which they live is one in which non-psychiatrists can issue prescriptions for medications. Such ignorance is not helpful to the cause of making the deliverance ministry more mainstream. To any mental health professional reading this book, I say, "We need each other!" We need to incorporate every reasonable (non-occult) healing modality available to bring wholeness to the collective, fractured soul of our society. And this would include elevating the role of exorcism to a respected spiritual art which, when it is practiced intelligently and reasonably, can be incorporated as a helping hand to the mental health community.

PERSPECTIVE

Our International School of Exorcism has an entire course exploring this matter of understanding the spiritual intersection of body, soul, and spirit. One of the most important topics discussed is the contrasting viewpoints of what's known as "traducianism" versus "soul-creation." Traducianism teaches that the soul and body come from one's own parents; just as the body is generated by the parent, so is the soul. Thus there is a clear path to understanding the inheritance of family traits and generational curses. Soul-creationism promotes the idea that each soul is a direct creation of God. Admittedly, Church Fathers differed on their interpretations of these doctrines. For example, Tertullian favored traducianism while St. Augustine wasn't as convinced. Were these esteemed teachers of church doctrine to encounter the plethora of demonic possession cases we face today, often energized by generational curses, they might well be more inclined to the traducian viewpoint. Contemporary theologians such as Lewis

Sperry Chafer, Gordon Clark, and Norman Geisler support the traducian viewpoint. Catholics generally hold to the soul-creation view while many Protestants, most notably Lutherans, are traducian in belief.

This theological matter is too profound and complex to discuss here in brief. But considering the idea that souls are not created directly, but rather generated by one's ancestors, is more consistent with what we discover in deliverance ministry. In the Old Testament, for example, the soul of an individual was considered to be present in the "loins" of the ancestor. (See Hebrews 7:10, for example, which refers to a child yet unborn: "he was still in the loins of his father.") Please note that my book *Jezebel: Defeating Your #1 Spiritual Enemy* deals at length with the matter of Genesis chapter 6 and the Nephilim (chapter 15). If some demons did cohabit with humans to produce a mongrelized offspring, traducianism more easily explains this monstrous phenomenon.

Why is this topic important to a perspective on this chapter? Once we establish a clear ancestral path of inheriting soul/body deficiencies, both physical and mental, we see why understanding the mind/body connection is so important. Traducianism also explains a lot about how the tendency toward generational mental illnesses is inherited. Sleuthing the connections between body and soul makes more sense if we understand that there can be a demonic continuum, unbroken, generation to generation, without active spiritual intervention. What each new generation receives in the body or soul has a profound relationship to the fallen human family, and in particular the evil of one's forebears.

NOTE

1. Gina Shaw, "New Study Suggests Brain Is Connected to the Lymphatic System," *Neurology Today,* 2 July 2015, Vol. 15, Issue 13, pp. 1, 9–10 (http://journals.lww.com/neurotodayonline/Fulltext/2015/07020/New_Study _Suggests_Brain_Is_Connected_to_the.1.aspx).

Chapter Seven

SECOND THAT EMOTION

ANDREW AND HEATHER APPEARED TO BE THE QUINTESSENTIAL Christian couple, but they were having a challenging family crisis. They scheduled a Personal Spiritual Encounter session with me to discuss problems they faced with their 16-year-old son, Todd. The young man had suddenly turned sullen, had experimented with drugs, and had come home drunk several times after staying out beyond curfew. He had lost interest in church and only went when forced to do so. His younger sister, Rebecca, aged 13, was also showing signs of rebellion, talking back and dropping the occasional F-bomb, language never permitted at home.

Andrew and Heather described themselves as straight-laced, evangelical Christians with a charismatic bent. They seemed genuinely puzzled why Todd's life had taken such a sudden turn away from

God. They insisted to me that Todd's behavior was contrary to all the values they had tried to instill in him. He'd had the best of private Christian schools, summer church youth camps, and had even gone on a church mission to Central America. To their knowledge he hadn't gotten mixed up with the wrong crowd. He didn't even have a girlfriend who might be leading him astray. How had this crisis arisen?

The youth pastor of their church had tried talking with Todd, without success. They had taken him to a Christian counselor, but Todd refused to go back after just a few sessions. Even Heather, who seemed most tuned in to the situation, felt like the counselor was treading water and not doing much to change things. In a situation like this, who're you gonna call?

I've often described our healing and deliverance ministry as the knot at the end of people's rope, that last place they turn when all the conventional Christian wisdom has failed. It shouldn't be that way, but face it: for most mainstream Christians, the idea that one's behavior could be demonically driven is a bit too far out. Still, I'm glad to be there when everything else has been exhausted. And this is where Andrew and Heather found themselves, with nowhere else to turn.

THE HEART CANNOT LIE

As we talked, I asked to see the Personal Profile forms that both Andrew and Heather had filled out before scheduling this session. Andrew handed me the paperwork, but I could see that he was a bit defensive. He voiced his thoughts firmly.

"I don't see why Heather and I had to fill out these forms," Andrew objected. "You already have Todd's paperwork. He's the one with the problems. And one more thing. Why did you ask to talk to me and Heather first? We don't have a lot of time to see you, and we really need you to work with Todd and get him fixed."

I wasn't surprised at the reaction. I'd seen it before, and it told me volumes. I took a breath to calm my response and looked at Andrew seriously.

"Let me put it to you bluntly. When I hear of a situation like this I almost always assume that before there was a kid problem, there was a parent problem."

Andrew was taken aback by my bluntness. I continued.

"Please understand, I'm not looking for fault; I'm looking for facts. This isn't about whether you two have been good or bad parents. It's about to what extent Todd's problems are a reflection of the family dynamics."

Andrew remained tense. Heather reached over and took his hand as if to preemptively calm a possible angry reaction.

I went on. "If you told me that Todd had been sexually violated or that one of you had physically abused him with your disciplinary habits, I might see the obvious smoking gun I'm looking for. That's not the case. I've looked at his profile, and there's no evidence of bullying or mistreatment of any kind. I accept the fact that you two believe that you did everything possible to raise him in what you believed to be a good Christian environment. But when I see a case like this I operate on a basic principle: Good parenting usually produces good kids, while bad parenting often produces troubled kids. In fact, the issue may not be how you treated Todd but how you have treated each other."

I could see that Andrew was doing a slow boil inside. This isn't what he wanted to hear. Heather was equally uncomfortable; one of her eyes was starting to water with emotion.

I gestured toward Todd's profile in my hands and the places I had circled his responses to certain personal characteristics. "Assuming he filled this out accurately, he indicates strong feelings of worthlessness, insecurity, and low self-esteem. He's checked off that he's filled with rage and unforgiveness. He even has thoughts of self-harm. He has honestly indicated that he's depressed and suicidal. That's not the picture of a child who's the product of a loving, spiritually healthy family."

Heather squeezed Andrew's hand tightly as if to restrain him from reacting to what I was saying.

"Let me pose a few simple questions. How often does Todd see the two of you express genuine affection for one another? Seldom? Never? Heather, you answer, please."

Heather's voice was shaking. "Well, we used to…"

She began to slowly weep. "That was until Andrew…"

I thought that any minute Andrew would bolt from the room. To his credit, he didn't.

"Did what?"

"You tell him, Andrew," Heather insisted.

Andrew spoke softly. "A couple of years ago I got involved with another woman. It was brief. We didn't even have sex but it was enough to push me and Heather apart. Since then we haven't…"

"Been intimate," I finished the sentence. "And my guess is that it's not just the sex that's missing, it's also open displays of affection between the two of you."

Both nodded in agreement.

I challenged them rhetorically. "And you really think your kids aren't picking up on that? Todd probably lacks confidence because you two aren't secure with each other. He's depressed because you two are depressed in your relationship. He can't be emotionally intimate with you when you two aren't physically and emotionally intimate with each other. Plus, he's angry and really doesn't know why, but he's acting out that anger in self-destructive ways."

I could see that tears were also filling Andrew's eyes.

"Like I said, we have a parent problem that's at the root of Todd's problems." I glanced at Andrew's profile. "I see that you didn't get along with your dad, and you describe the relationship as bad. How bad?"

"Bad. Real bad. He was never there for me, ever. He was always too busy. I suppose that's why my mom got fed up and divorced him."

"And you were how old at the time?"

"About 10 or 11," Andrew said.

I saw a flash of anger in his eyes and detected a slight twitch on his check. Something didn't like the direction I was going. And that something was evil.

I cut to the chase. "I'm glad you all came to see me, but to be honest I don't think Todd is the one with demons. He certainly has behavioral issues, but someone else has the demons."

Andrew exploded. He jumped to his feet and bolted for the door. I blocked the way, and intensely looked him in the eye. "I know you're there, Satan," I blurted out definitely. "You want to destroy this man, his marriage, and his kids. Well, you're not going to do it."

I aggressively pressed my Bible against Andrew's chest. The demonic response was instant. "He's mine. His dad was mine. All the men in his bloodline were mine. And his son is mine, too. He's so pathetic he doesn't even know what finally drove his mom to leave his dad."

"Adultery?"

The demon laughed. "Yeah, and I'll get this guy, too. Just give me time."

Andrew's exorcism proceeded, much along the lines of the others you've read in this book. What's crucial to note is the way I had to expose the real problem. To the parents, the dilemma seemed simple: their children, especially their son, were having behavioral issues. Fix the kids, and everything would be OK. Obviously, not so. Between husband and wife, there are often subtle interplays of implicit, unspoken brokenness that lead to bad emotional health where their offspring are concerned.

The task of an effective deliverance minister is to get to the source of the fundamental demonic stronghold, which is often masked by overt, symptomatic expressions that are bellwethers, rather than causes. The truth concerning what's wrong in most families is often found in the hidden realms of the soul, where what an individual really thinks or feels is obscured.

As it turned out, Todd's problems were primarily a reflection of his parents' unwillingness to face their own "demons." Though they looked good on the outside, in the soul realm neither Andrew nor Heather was emotionally healthy. Further investigation revealed that Andrew was raised by an austere, emotionally distant father who practiced harsh discipline. Few parenting skills were modeled in the home. Andrew had never known unconditional acceptance, and consequently he had little capacity to affirm Todd in meaningful ways. The pre-puberty divorce of his parents further eroded any ability to understand what an emotionally healthy home looked like.

Heather's situation, it turns out, was similar. Her mother had enabled the abusive actions of her husband, Heather's father, by failing to intervene and provide an emotional safe place for Heather. So, when Andrew acted injuriously, she had no healthy boundaries to resist and demand proper treatment for her and her children. When he strayed from his marriage vows, Heather didn't know how to insist upon being treated with integrity. Her mother had been compliant to mistreatment, and it was thus easier for Heather to keep silent than to risk blowing up the marriage. Todd was caught in the middle of all this.

HOW DO YOU REALLY FEEL ABOUT THAT?

One of the most critical aspects of counseling, and certainly deliverance, is assessing the emotional health of the client. How a person feels is crucial to understanding his or her potential for spiritual liberation. At this point, we need to pause and consider the spirit/body/soul matrix and the part that the soul plays in demonization. I have written about this topic in several of my books, and our International School of Exorcism contains detailed explanations regarding how this tripartite aspect of the human condition functions and how the components interact. My definitions here are simple and not intended to be exhaustive.

The spirit is the eternal, God-breathed part of each person. The body is the human encasement of all physical actions and sensations. The soul is the individuated aspect of each human being, the sentient, self-perceptual part of who we each are, and that which identifies us as unique, one-of-a-kind creations of God. Scripture teaches that all the parts of human life operate most effectively when in every way they are spiritually surrendered to God. As Paul told the Thessalonians, "May the God of peace Himself sanctify you completely; and may your whole spirit, soul, and body be preserved blameless at the coming of our Lord Jesus Christ" (1 Thessalonians 5:23). Thus, spirit, soul, and body are separate components of the human condition, together comprising the triune nature of man.

The soul, or "psyche" in the Greek, is the seat of our emotions, the fount of our feelings, the crucible of our thoughts, and the essence of our minds. The will is like a switch located between the intersection of the soul and the spirit, and can bend in either direction. Our will may follow the leading of the spirit (see Romans 8:14) or the impulses of the soul (see Romans 8:5–6).

Demons cannot enter the spirit of the eternally reborn child of God. They may invade the body and create physical infirmities. But our purpose in this chapter is to explore how evil spirits penetrate and embed in the mind/soul of an individual. This is their most frequent place of haunting the life of a Christian. And it is here that demons build the strongholds spoken of in Second Corinthians 10:4. Simply put, a "stronghold" is a place of emotional embedment in the mind where demonic forces have captured one or more aspect of consciousness. To some extent these evil introjections are influencing or misdirecting thoughts, feelings, and emotions in an ungodly direction.

Strictly speaking, there is no such thing as a negative emotion. There are just emotions. It is the contextualization of emotions that quantifies them morally. Take anger, for example. Psalm 7:11 tells us that God is angry with the wicked. Christ drove the money changers from the temple because the "zeal" (anger) of the Lord compelled Him (see Matthew 21:12–13 and John 2:17). Even hate can have a godly function. Luke 16:13 reminds us that we are to love God and hate the demonic forces that would turn us from Him.

A stronghold develops when Satan takes a healthy emotion and turns it into a destructive force. How a person really feels about a situation determines whether the good or evil aspects of a particular emotion may become a demonic stronghold.

Over time I have developed a template that categorizes human behavior into groupings that allow me to quickly assess the emotional state of a person. I catalogue them as follows:

- Negative self-assessments

- Anger issues

- Death preoccupations

- Aberrational behavior (including addictions, criminal actions, and mental disorders)

Obviously, there are many more categories that we might have included; but for the sake of brevity, these four will suffice as a model for other behavioral considerations. We'll take a brief look at each category and determine why it is important. I'll also explain how and where demons hide in and manipulate each particular classification. We'll discuss ways to bring healing and resolution so that evil spirits can no longer exploit the wounded parts of the soul that are stuck in unhealthy bondages.

Negative Self-Assessments

I often ask people to give me a single word that best describes the state of their internal, emotional world. When I hear words like "depressed," "insecure," "anxious," or "worthless," I take note. Esteem is the way in which we regard something, usually high or low. When it is personal self-esteem that is negative (as mirrored by words such as those noted above) it usually points to a lack of significant regard an individual has felt. The negating messages may have come from peers, teachers, classmates, or siblings. But when it is fostered from the top down by a parent, it is especially damaging. If a child's grades are never good enough for Mom, or performance on the playing field always gets a put-down from Dad, the child sees the world as adversarial. Each task becomes yet another impossible hurdle.

Unfortunately, an observable rule of psychology is that we all tend to adapt negative external assessments more quickly than positive ones; therefore, a parent may make a dozen hopeful statements to a child but have it all undone by one harsh word spoken in anger or frustration. This leads to shaming, which then results in depressed and insecure self-perceptions. Sometimes these self-damaging emotions go beyond creating fear and social reluctance to more damaging addictive and narcissistic behavior.

The voiced opinion of a parent is the most consequential feedback a child receives. Those who understand demonic strategy, as I do, immediately recognize an opening for all kinds of spiritual oppression in the life of a negatively self-assessed person who, as a child, was not reasonably affirmed at home.

To weaken the demonic grasp on the mind of such individuals, you must get them to see that a bad self-perception, motivated by the unhealthy opinion of an unwise or emotionally unhealthy person (even a parent), is not valid. If one's mother was raised in a dysfunctional home, her parenting skills may be lacking; thus, her constant berating may say more about her childhood home life than it does about the actions of her own child. When a child acts in a self-punishing way the behavior may be based on accepting a false judgment coming from a parent who doesn't have an adequate understanding of his or her own behavioral problems. It's important for deliverance clients to know that God's scriptural opinion of them is the one that matters most. They must be affirmed that Christ welcomes them just as they are, as the father did his prodigal son (see Luke 15). Whatever our weaknesses and failures, we are "accepted in the Beloved" (Ephesians 1:6).

As human beings we tend to act out the ways that we see ourselves. Individuals who have absorbed many years, sometimes a lifetime, of negative input from significant people in their lives are deeply wounded and often incapable of declaring emotional truth. They will then think of themselves as inferior, unacceptable, and worthy of only self-condemnation. Since the devil doesn't want us to see ourselves as loved and embraced by God, demons will seize on this way of thinking to amplify and intensify it.

In the case of Andrew and Heather above, their children absorbed the strained and tense behavior of their parents toward each other. No one had to say anything; it was felt in the emotional environment of the home. The barely hidden animosity their mom and dad felt in their relationship made Todd and his sister feel lacking in their own self-confidence. And because parents are destined by God to be the protectors of their children, lack of proper parental spiritual oversight gives Satan the right to adversely oppress the offspring. It didn't help that Andrew was also demonized because of generational curses.

A good place to start ministry with those who have negative self-assessments is my book *Demon Proofing Prayers*, which contains many positive affirmations of spiritual health. These declarations are in the forms of prayers which can be recited over and over to reinforce the divine perspective of our human condition. In addition, I encourage people to read the Bible with the intent of noting those verses which speak best to them in encouraging ways. Examples would be the idea of being seated in "heavenly places" (Ephesians 1:3) with Christ and being relationally bound to the Lord in such a way that nothing may "separate us from the love of Christ" (Romans 8:35).

I don't often quote questionable secular sources to correct demonically exploited behavior, but consider this interesting observation of psychologist Carl Jung. (To learn more about errors in the teaching of Jung, the International School of Exorcism has several courses devoted to understanding the intersection of psychological insights and the perspective of Christian theology.) Jung declared, "Until you make the unconscious the conscious it will direct your life and you will call it fate." I'd like to paraphrase that slightly, in the context of this book: *Until you uncover, and face, the erroneous self-assessments which are unconsciously guiding your life, you may take them for truth and without intention open the door to spiritual oppression.*

Anger Issues

When prospective deliverance clients tell me they have anger issues, I always want to know more specifically the expression that rage takes. Is it slow-boil anger, or hair-trigger explosiveness? Is it rooted in envy, jealousy? How much bitterness and revenge-seeking is part of the anger? Does it verge on hatred and the desire for intentional, get-even harm to others? Is it outright, unmitigated rage? And, perhaps the most important question is this: "Is it attached to harbored feelings of being unwilling to forgive the wrongdoer?" What I'm looking for is the range of the anger—from minor irritation to full-blown demonic fury. How have demons interfered to make a small annoyance into a relationship-threatening obsession?

Taken in a positive perspective, anger can spur action to right a grievance caused by an injustice, but unhealthy anger usually feeds on a real or perceived wrong from another person, and out-of-control anger can have many ill consequences. It may affect blood pressure and overall health; it can lead to mental illness; it often destroys marriages and the bond between a parent and child; it can become a compulsion that overrides reason and sound judgment, leading to bad decisions of all kinds. Most important, it may drive an individual away from God, especially if that anger is directed toward the Lord. Worse yet it could go beyond a human frailty to become the habitation of an evil spirit whose sole function is to further heighten the anger until it is an all-consuming destructive force.

In short, the deliverance minister needs to ascertain whether the anger is an emotion of the "flesh" to be disciplined, a resident demon exploiting some internal soul weakness and needing to be cast out, or a little of both. In making that determination it's helpful to know more about the full range of anger and what motivates it.

Usually, anger isn't calculated. It's reactive, often occurring as a result of physical or mental pain inflicted by a person or situation. It may occur without an external stimulus, such as when it comes from internal feelings of disregard. Anger is not present unless it is triggered by something. Even when we say that so-and-so is "an angry person" we are only describing what they have become, not what they were intrinsically, in most cases. An exception would be an individual demonized from birth who was born with a curse due to some precipitating anger in an ancestor.

Here is what's crucial. Destructive anger isn't isolated. It must give rise to some adverse thought. And usually that thought is rooted in false assumptions. It is the untruthful assessment of what someone has done that causes unjustifiable anger. Getting the client to see that he or she may be filled with anger because of erroneous assumptions is a big step toward healing and demonic dislodgment. Suppose the internalized conclusion is that "Mom always favored my big sister." Anger toward the mother or sister, or both, if given time to percolate, can become a demonic obsession; but what if that conclusion just isn't true? Talking to other family members who see things differently can help to diffuse the bitterness.

Anger almost always is directed at someone or something. Find out what or who that is. (A person can even be angry at him- or herself and be consumed with self-hate.) Often the injury is perceived, not real. For example, another sibling may point out that Mother didn't, in fact, favor big sister. That's how the individual saw it because of other emotional circumstances in the home. Confronting the false conclusions that led to the anger, or dealing with the paranoia associated with it, can undercut what demonic forces may be telling the person to reinforce the lie. Demons are good at inventing things in the mind of the host and blowing small slights into major life-defining moments.

Anger can also be a trick of the mind, sometimes facilitated by demons, to misdirect attention from the real problem. Suppose that an individual was sexually molested as a child. Anger may effectively wall off the memory of the abuse. Being mad at everyone and anyone makes it possible to avoid facing the pain and receiving healing; it's an emotional distraction. It may even be invested in a dissociative, multiple personality state that holds the anger and becomes defined by the anger. This is often seen with self-harming individuals who may cut or injure themselves to misdirect the internal pain. This transmutation shifts the focus of the anger from outward expression, which can be socially unacceptable, to a self-inflicted focus.

Often anger is a form of self-protection. When an individual doesn't want to deal with a fear or an emotionally intolerable situation (again, such as sexual abuse) the real source of internal torment is projected outwardly to whatever is irritable at the moment. Encountering an angry deliverance client is an opportunity to probe more deeply into hidden or repressed circumstances that initially he or she may be unwilling to face; and it is there that the demonic place of attachment is found. Resolving the anger issue with spiritual inner healing may remove the need for outward expressions of bitterness and also cancel a demonic right for evil spirits to maintain their internalization.

Death Preoccupation

At times the deliverance minister may encounter people who are obsessed with thoughts of death, suicide, and various forms of self-destruction. For the moment we'll set aside the issue of how mental illness affects one's view of life and death and consider first the preoccupation some have with death and dying.

Shakespeare's *Hamlet* may seem like a strange place to begin, but fans of the English bard will recall that the play is saturated with thoughts of death. It begins with the ghost of Hamlet's father introducing the moribund topic. The main characters succumb to death one by one: Polonius, Gertrude, Ophelia, et al. Thus we see that, although the obsession about death and dying are nothing new, what's unique today is the prevalence of such thinking, even in an era of expanded health care for formerly fatal diseases and the growth of the psychological sciences to treat all manner of unsound thinking.

In America, arguably one of the most advanced civilizations in history, there are an estimated one million suicide attempts annually. According to the American Foundation for Suicide Prevention, 40,000 attempts are successful, making suicide the tenth leading cause of death in the United States. Among those aged 10–24 it is the second leading cause of death. Of those who die by suicide, 90 percent had a diagnosable psychiatric disorder at the time of their death.

To be preoccupied with death is to have it overtake one's thinking to the point of excluding most other positive thoughts. Death takes up an outsized portion of emotional energy, moving beyond the depressed "I wish I were dead" or "I wish I had never been born" to actively envisioning one's own funeral. Despair and hopelessness give way to emotional indifference, withdrawal, and a sense that nothing gives pleasure anymore, not even formerly enjoyable activities.

When a deliverance minister encounters such thinking, it may be necessary to immediately refer the person to mental health professionals for stabilizing medication. Even information about a suicide hotline might be in order. As to intervention with prayers of deliverance, that assessment has to be made based on how intense the death-thinking may be and whether it characterizes the rest of the client's demeanor. People who otherwise are "normal" in their outlook, whom friends testify are usually upbeat, may either be suffering psychologically (e.g., bipolar disorder or major clinical depression) or from spiritual oppression—or both.

The purpose of this book is not to take the place of clinical advice or intervention, but rather to consider the spiritual ramifications of a death obsession. Consequently, consider these factors which may point in the direction of concluding that there is demonic influence:

- Has some history of occult involvement opened the door to spirits of death? Prior experiences with an Ouija board or dabbling in witchcraft may have allowed a death demon to enter.

- Was the onset of the preoccupation with death rather sudden, possibly triggered by some abuse trauma? Or was it slow? Mental health usually deteriorates gradually over a period of time. There is gradual and long trajectory to emotional disintegration. Demonic thoughts of death come on more quickly, often after specific events that are common demonic entry experiences, such as rape or violent physical assault.

- Is talk of death or suicide triggered (incongruously) by spiritual discussions, worship, church attendance, or being in religious settings? When a person is around life-affirming and eternity-reinforcing activities, which should provide a hopeful outlook, death ideas would seem to be out of place. If a Christian environment doesn't mitigate the problem, demons may be reacting to combat positive spiritual influences. Remember according to Jesus, Satan comes to steal, destroy, and kill (see John 10:10).

- When friends and family challenge the ideas of death, is there an odd reaction of defiance that might be rooted in a demonically controlled alter-ego state of consciousness? Multiple personalities, as discussed later in this chapter and detailed extensively in our International School of Exorcism, may include an alter-ego state with a death agenda that is not shared by the person's Christian-committed consciousness. (Evil spirits can hide in a dissociative identity fragment of the soul and influence thinking despite the belief system of the spiritually reborn core identity.)

- Has proper medication and psychological assistance failed to relieve the problem? If death desires persist after therapeutic intervention, the problem may have more of a spiritual (demonic) component.

- When the person speaks of wanting to die, do the spiritual consequences of such a wish enter into the conversation? The Christian believer contemplating suicide may have thoughts ranging from the belief that killing one's self leads to eternal damnation to the opinion that self-inflicted harm is unforgiveable in this life. If the individual seems detached from any theological significance to their actions (e.g., fear of damnation), the case for demonization is more probable.

- Is there a pattern of sinful behavior (e.g., drug-taking, extensive sexual promiscuity, antisocial behavior) leading up to the death thoughts, which might indicate a behavioral demonic opening? These kinds of sinful behaviors are doorways for demons, especially true if extensive. Satan will use guilt, self-condemnation, and a sense of futility to induce hopelessness, leading to the idea that death might be preferable.

- When the individual is confronted with the biblical view of death, perhaps via quotation of relevant Scriptures, do you detect an evil edge to the death-affirming outlook? If Christian counseling and the encouraging input of friends and loved ones do not help, then an exorcism may be in order.

- Has the death-obsessed individual had an abortion, which may point to the invasion of a spirit of Murder or Death? Such demons may enter not only the woman who sought the abortion but also her lover/spouse who consented to the abortion. This sin must be repented of and renounced, and all curses of death broken, as explained in my book *Curse Breaking.*

- Are any of the death wishes directed outward; does the person wish to harm another individual? Mental health factors and biological/hormonal imbalances may cause depression leading to death obsessions, but this may not explain an intent to harm others. Any time someone wishes death on friends, family, or even random individuals, it is more likely that the problem is demonic.

- Is the death wish accompanied by self-injurious behavior, such as cutting? Many factors can lead to purposefully hurting one's own body, and one factor is an internalized demon of destruction. For example, a cutter who isn't looking so much to self-punish or to expunge internalized psychological pain may be engaging in demonically generated, death-defying actions.

- Are death wishes connected to addictions (alcohol, drugs, pornography)? The inability of an individual to overcome the bondage of addiction may lead to hopelessness, and death may seem like a quick fix to end the internal conflict. Demons seize upon the despair and twist the addiction-addled mind into believing that killing oneself is somehow a noble way out of the predicament.

Aberrational Behavior

The range of "aberrational" behavior exhibited by a prospective deliverance client is quite broad. For our purposes, this classification will include any actions which deviate from the normal behavior expected of a socially well-adjusted person. In someone who has declared a Christian confession, aberrational actions include departures from normative biblical boundaries, encompassing mental irregularities that reflect something other than a sound mind. The basic categories of behavior we'll consider include the following:

- Eating disorders

- Compulsive disorders

- Addictions

- Criminal actions

- Dissociative identity disorder (DID) (popularly called multiple personality disorder, or MPD)

Please note that I have not included any diagnosable mental disorders such as major depressive disorder, bipolar disorder, borderline schizophrenia, and such. I have covered these thoroughly in our International School of Exorcism. In addition, what we've included here and in the School is by no means intended to be a professional clinical analysis. Clients with severely troubled conditions should always be referred to proper assistance from mental health care professionals. In some cases, psychological and neurological testing may be needed, as well as appropriate medication for the most severe cases which do not respond to spiritual ministry.

However, there is another reality that must be faced. Many people who seek the help of deliverance ministers fall into two particular categories: (1) they are not aware of the kinds of emotional help that may be available, and (2) they may for various reasons be unwilling to seek professional help, especially if it is secular. These oppositions may be due to ignorance, religious prejudices, or fear of exposing their vulnerabilities. Many people, especially Christians, are fearful of the medical establishment, especially the therapeutic community. They may not want to be medicated, having heard horror stories of those who were mentally zombified by drug-pumping doctors who listened little and prescribed much. (Believe me, I've seen too much of that.)

A major hurdle to getting people the right kind of help is an unfounded prejudice within the evangelical Christian community—the idea that all "shrinks" are intent on being dismissive of sincerely-held Christian values and will automatically oppose what the client believes. True, there are many New Age and nontheistic clinicians, but in my experience, most are motivated by a sincere desire to alleviate human emotional suffering and will try to accommodate the patient's convictions unless they run contrary to the best interests of the therapy.

As we look more closely at aberrational behavior, keep in mind that these are not exhaustive descriptions, just brief surveys. Much additional information is available online for further research. My intent is to improve general awareness of these problems as they may be encountered during the process of inner healing, deliverance, and exorcism.

In other words, this is not intended to be a professional guide to understanding and treating these aberrational behaviors, which should be left to mental health care experts, but rather a layman's guide to confronting these issues as they arise in healing prayer ministry. It's a "good neighbor" approach to providing emotional and spiritual support and offering such help as the non-credentialed deliverance minister may provide.

In reality, some individuals in desperate need either can't find a mental health professional or they flat-out refuse to see one, spiritualizing all their symptoms. This book can provide some direction in these situations if it can at least get tormented souls to recognize that they need knowledgeable intervention, and they can learn about some of the ways that evil spirits exploit human difficulties to bring spiritual bondage.

Eating Disorders

The best known eating disorders are anorexia and bulimia. Whatever the particular disorder, whether starving oneself (anorexia nervosa) or binging on food and then purging or regurgitating it (bulimia nervosa), or another abnormal eating habit, it eventually affects both physical and mental health. Compulsive exercising, sometimes indulged in to the point of exhaustion, may be part of the disorder, connecting self-worth to athletic prowess. Some individuals may be obsessed with eating only certain kinds of food in cyclical extremes. Depression, hormonal disorders, addictions, and suicidal ideation may accompany such situations. Social isolation is typical, in particular the avoidance of those who do not share the food obsession. Whatever the disorder, it can be life-threatening.

Our concern within the parameters of this book is to determine to what extent demonization is involved. Since a root cause of eating aberrations is often abuse of some kind, especially sexual abuse, the disorder may be more than the expression of an emotional problem. Demons may be hiding behind the symptoms, seeking to destroy, even kill, the individual. Eating disorders may be rooted in self-hatred due to a skewed idea of diminished personal worth. It may also be a form of self-punishment, a feeling of not being good enough, especially if the person was raised in a demanding home where acceptance was based on performance. Depending on the severity of the condition at the time it is brought to the deliverance minister, immediate medical attention may be in order. I have encountered very severe cases in which I insisted on a doctor's intervention before I would proceed with deliverance prayers. Other times I refused to minister to people unless they agreed to also see a health professional who deals with the clinical aspects of eating issues.

Compulsive Disorders

Compulsive behavior has the potential to be a subtle, but very destructive, form of behavior that may give strong clues to the presence of evil spirits. In the most simple forms, such as nail-biting, cutting, obsessive-compulsive behavior, gambling, tics, burning, or repetitive washing, to name a few, the intent is to refocus internal emotional and spiritual chaos to some artificial, external criterion that can be controlled. For example, inner emotional pain of past abuse, unresolved by therapy and inner healing, will come out as an addiction or compulsion. (In many addictions, individuals are rewarding themselves by receiving some stimulus.)

Shopping, hoarding, skin-picking, hair-pulling (trichotillo-mania), and sexual addiction are other examples of compulsive behavior. Individuals raised in perfectionist homes may never feel good enough to please their parents, so they develop fixations with something that is within their control, such as repeating certain tasks (such as hand-washing) over and over to demonstrate that they are, at last, in control. In ministry I've encountered people who were obsessed with colors, words, and even numbers. One Encounter client would have anxiety attacks in a restaurant if the bill came to certain numbers, or if while driving he saw a certain license plate with specific number sequences. The seeming loss of control brought on the stress reaction.

As with many similar disorders, the underlying genesis is usually traumatic. And where you find unresolved trauma, demons aren't far behind. This isn't to say that all obsessive-compulsive-disordered (OCD) people are demonized, but the likelihood is substantially increased. On another level, I've counseled compulsive people who used their disorder to manipulate others, threating to cut, go into fits of rage, engage in socially destructive behavior, or indulge in sexually risky actions if they didn't get their way. Thus, compulsions may be both an expression of internal torment as well as a means of seeking to manage hidden fears and terrorizing memories.

Things may get dangerous if a compulsion characterized by violent or erratic thoughts compels someone to act out. It takes skill and spiritual discernment to understand when such actions are behaviorally manipulative and when they are demonic characteristics. The best way to find the truth is to challenge the behavior on all levels, seeking not only to reorder the behavior but also to uncover the underlying lies. If the deliverance minister is loving and patient yet firm in not indulging compulsions, there may be demonic push-back which uncovers the underlying demonization. As the minister pushes through the myths (e.g., "If I cut myself I'll be in control of my pain"; "If I bathe 10 times a day I'll never be ill"; "If I walk a certain number of steps every day..."), the truth will win out and evil will be exposed. The compulsive person must be introduced to the idea that true happiness is portrayed in Christ's Sermon on the Mount (Matthew 6), especially in the "do not worry" verses (25 through 34).

Always keep in mind that compulsive disorders are generally shame-based and that it takes time to jettison the disabling emotions attached to guilt and false guilt, learning to regulate emotions and avoid the "I have to be perfect" trap. One of the best ways is by having a close circle of affirming friends who are part of a solid Christian fellowship. Such associations will be especially helpful if there is a relapse to the false security found in compulsions.

If, however, an evil spirit is embedded, that demon must be dislodged for all other aspects of healing to be effective. If an evil spirit of Destruction or Self-Destruction is present, don't hesitate to confront it boldly. Removing the supernatural source of the lies that undergird the compulsion will enable the person to think more clearly and establish the boundaries necessary for living a compulsion-free life.

Addictions

You can find a wealth of information online about facing and defeating various addictions, so I will not rehash it here. My purpose in this section is to focus on the nature of addictions as they relate to demonization. Addiction is not limited to alcohol or drug abuse. Gambling, pornography, eating, and even destructive relationships can be equally addictive. What's common to all addictions is the pleasure principle—some perceived benefit from the indulgence.

From a deliverance perspective, we understand that addictions can be the direct result of an actual demon of addiction that drives the behavior. Also, the addiction may lead to demonization which essentially places any remedy beyond sheer will power to stop.

To consider how demons use the addictive process, here are some basic facts about how addictions emotionally operate. Here are some indicators:

- Frequent engagement with the destructive behavior, more than occasional indulgence.

- Enjoyment of the gratification without regard for consequences.

- Sneaky, clandestine participation with high risk that brings a thrill.

- Management of withdrawal symptoms such as a hangover with greater dosages of the addictive substance.

- Narcissistic denial that anyone else is being harmed.

- An internalized conclusion that life would be unbearable without the dependency.

These indicators operate in compulsive ways as long as some apparently discernible reward seems to outweigh the consequences of the negative effects upon health, relationships, and spiritual values. For our purposes, we'll not deal with the biochemical and neurological aspects of addiction. Our concern is with behavioral addiction.

Once again, drawing from my wealth of experience working with people in various stages of addiction, from teenagers experimenting with weed to older adults whose lives have been shattered by the subordination of all normal human desires to the quest for the addictive substance/actions, I propose to answer a fundamental question: "When is an addiction just an addiction, and when is it demonically controlled or sustained?" The answer usually isn't either/or, but a combination.

What rehabilitation experts call an "addictive personality" may be an observable generational curse in action. The tendency to sedate personal pain or medicate wounded emotions may be learned during childhood by being raised in a home where alcohol, for example, greases the wheels of emotional survival; when it's endemic to the family structure, it's an invitation to demons. The parent who abuses drugs is inviting evil spirits to torment his or her child with similar inclinations, and this can include outright possession by a spirit of Addiction. The task of the deliverance minister is to sort through this perfect storm of dysfunction, leaving what is behaviorally remediable to the rehab experts and focusing on getting out the demons that won't allow any clinical intervention to work.

Here are some tips; here's how I approach the typical situation by asking these questions:

"How many generations have struggled with addiction?" The more generations, the more likely there is a spiritual root to the problem.

"How have attempts to reform included therapy, rehab, or professional intervention?" Many cases come to me after a lengthy attempt to solve the problem with counseling. One female addict told me that one of our Encounter sessions accomplished what $20,000 in drug counseling programs had failed to achieve. The driving force was demons, and I was the first one to intervene at that level.

"How desperate are you to be free? Desperate enough to consider an exorcism?" One family brought to me their bright, handsome, highly educated son who was a heroin addict. They had spent more than $40,000 on therapy, but he was still no better. In one day of deliverance, he was totally set free and is still clean today.

The family was desperate enough to consider an extreme spiritual solution: confronting evil spirits trying to destroy this young man.

"How long has the addiction been going on, and what progressions have there been to harder drugs?" I attempt to assess how deeply the addiction is entrenched and to what extent profound behavioral modification may be necessary to precede spiritual healing.

"What relationships inside and outside the family have reinforced the addiction?" Someone who has been raised in a family of addicts usually has a more demonized problem. The addiction is there not just because of the bad choices of the individual but also because of a systemic environment of substance dependency, a breeding ground for demons.

There are many other questions which might also be relevant, but these few examples illustrate my lines of questioning. Addictions seldom occur outside the framework of family dynamics. Also, they are not often isolated actions that happen apart from other dependent or self-medicating behaviors. Finding the connections between the client's and family members' collective history and aggregate actions gives a clue as to how the individual spun out of control. Addictions are almost always traceable to something sick at home or in the previous generations. And until that curse is broken, all attempts at restoration to normalcy will be frustrated.

Criminal Actions

Some deliverance clients find it uncomfortable to talk about the subject of criminal, even felonious, behavior, but it can't be overlooked. I want to know if the individual has ever been arrested or spent time in prison. Why? A criminal record may alert the deliverance minister to the possibility of being conned by a sincere-seeming client who may have a history, often learned during incarceration, of deliberately giving misleading answers to straightforward questions. Also the severity of the person's sentence may indicate the kinds of demons lurking.

For example, someone convicted of a violent act may be possessed by a spirit of Murder or Violence. The same goes for rape or sexual assault. There is a good chance that such a person was sexually abused and acted out as a perpetrator of the crimes he or she suffered. Any and all clues are helpful if they lead to an understanding of the root of antisocial actions. The line of questioning should not be accusatory or condemning, but rather investigative. The deliverance minister is on a forensic pursuit to determine why certain criminal actions were committed, with the intent of revealing a demonic opening. Also, when it comes to renouncing curses, the person should be urged to declare null and void the effects of criminality as well as to repent for the unlawful acts he or she engaged in.

As discussed above, it's important to consider to what extent demonic anger and rage motivated the criminal actions. It's also crucial for the deliverance minister to be aware of how to identify pathological behavior, which may be the result of demons. If the client has a history of acting in extreme ways that seem impossible for the person to control in spite of the harm caused, there should be concern. Do those who know the client describe him or her as acting in compulsive patterns with complete disregard for how others will be harmed? Does the person react in extreme ways not warranted by the situation, for instance becoming violent or abusive over small things? Is the client self-centered about the effect his or her actions have upon others to the point of almost total emotional detachment? Does the person seem uncaring about how others are injured by antisocial or criminal actions, behaving as if devoid of a discernible conscience?

We often use the words "pathological" and "liar" in the same breath, indicating people who think they can lie with impunity with no concern for the outcome of their prevarication. Such behavior may be purely psychological, a kind of psychosis in which the person has limited or little contact with reality; however, note that both "pathological" and "criminal" aptly describe the nature of demons. Having the client break generational curses or read passages of Scripture about mercy and forgiveness may be enough to arouse the demons underlying the pathology.

Just be aware that people who have broken the law in significant, repetitive ways may be exhibiting more than a criminal mindset. They may also be telegraphing an underlying spiritual oppression from a spirit of Rebellion or Lawlessness.

Dissociative identity disorder (DID). My books, *Larson's Book of Spiritual Warfare, Curse Breaking,* and *Jezebel,* all deal with this phenomenon. Likewise, our School of Exorcism treats the subject in detail; hence there is no need to repeat here what is clearly laid out elsewhere. I will only mention the most cursory aspects of DID in bullet form to give a basic understanding:

- DID is popularly known by the designation MPD, multiple personality disorder, although today that term has been replaced in the American Psychological Association's approved *Diagnostic and Statistical Manual of Mental Disorders* by the designation "dissociative identity disorder."

- DID usually results from trauma which is so severe it is potentially disabling. The mind compartmentalizes the negative experience in an alter-ego, a state ("alter") that is often completely separate from conscious thinking and memories

- DID is not mental illness but rather a coping mechanism of the mind for emotional survival. It is the task of the alter who holds the memory to keep it hidden or removed from active thinking so as not to burden the conscious mind with often horrific, incapacitating thoughts. An alter is formed when there is nowhere to flee except inside the mind.

- Each alter identity maintains its own integrity of characteristics and habits, also often claiming its own name, age, personal tastes and even sexual identity. Alters may also have a spiritual belief system which is separate from, even antagonistic to, the core and most visibly present part of the person.

In deliverance it's important to recognize when an alter is "out," and presenting itself in a way separate from the person. Much harm can be done if an unaware deliverance minister mistakenly identifies an alter, especially an angry or violent one, as a demon and attempts to "cast" it out. Severe, even irreparable, emotional harm can be done. The alter may retreat from such an unwise confrontation and hide even deeper in the mind.

Demons regularly hide in alters for two reasons. First, the trauma which created the alter may have also opened a portal for demons to enter. Second, the presence of demons may be obscured because no one realizes that the person is suffering from DID and thus has no idea how to confront the demons residing only in certain alters.

Consider this case. A vibrant Christian woman seems to lead a successful spiritual life. Unbeknownst to outsiders, she may struggle with pornography or drug dependencies. What this woman never mentions is that she was molested as a child. At that time, she dissociated and her mind/soul created an alter to be the repository of the pain from the abuse. Most of the memories of the pain and shame are deposited there so the core person can go on with life. Unfortunately, the abuser may also have passed on demons at the time of the violation. And to make matters worse, a bitter, angry alter was formed that has no way to expunge the shame and thus turns to sexual indulgences and drug addictions. The path to this woman's freedom is to first bring emotional healing to the sexually violated alter and then cast out the demon which has cleverly hidden behind the dissociated smokescreen.

So much can be said about DID, but I've already pointed out our readily available resources. There are also many other fine books and blogs on the subject from clinicians and deliverance ministers. The competent exorcist will study this area assiduously. The reason? In my historical and professional opinion, more than half of all cases of demonization, particularly in the Western world, also involve dissociation of some degree. To set the captives free, the one who ministers in the name of Jesus must also know how to identify and resolve the fragmented emotions of the mind.

PERSPECTIVE

Please don't become overwhelmed by the intricacies of this chapter. I realize that to those new to deliverance ministry it may all seem to be overkill. It's not. Only a small part of the information in this chapter will be used at any given time in any particular case. But knowing that all these factors are to be considered at various times will alert the minister to reach back and glean each truth at the time of its particular application.

The strategies of demonic forces are far more complex than most imagine. And what I've written here is a small fraction of what I might have revealed. (But the rest is for another book and another time.) Just read and reread what is here and be aware of possible trails to go down when seeking to expose deeply rooted demons. Even one tactical bit of information in this chapter could be the key to a person's much-sought deliverance.

Satan would prefer that spiritual leaders take a more simplistic approach, overlooking the evil spirits that lurk in unsuspecting corners of the soul. Never underestimate the enemy and his use of the most elusive tactics to hold suffering souls in bondage. Determine that they will be set free by pursuing excellence and diligence when ferreting out the most ingenious of the devil's devices.

Our emotions are often a driving force in our behavior, influencing everything from how advertising affects us to our selection of friends and marital mates. Our work life, our social interactions, and our spiritual choices of theology and fellowship are often emotionally regulated. You may not think much about it, but the style of worship that most appeals to you and even the doctrinal persuasion you adopt are affected more by emotions than you realize. One's goals, passions, and proclivities are often driven more by emotions than logic or rationality. If you think that your decisions are mostly based on a cognitive appraisal of each situation, think again. Psychology and neuroscience now recognize that a predictive model of human behavior cannot omit serious consideration of the state of an individual's emotions.

When I asked above, "How do you really feel about that?" I wanted to introduce the reader to the idea that most forms of aberrational and self-destructive behavior are emotionally motivated. Whether one's emotions are overly focused on negativity, anger, or morbidity, how that person feels is what often determines how he or she acts. And for our purposes, at the root of unsanctified emotions is often a demonic stronghold. Remember, the legal rights that a demon claims are usually in the area of an individual's actions and choices, or those of his or her ancestors. But the stronghold is fixated on a wounded part of the soul where the heart suffers from past abuses and injustices.

Chapter Eight

CLOSING THE DEMON DOOR OF TRAUMA

I WOULD NOW LIKE TO ENGAGE THE READER ON A VERY PRACTICAL basis concerning how to understand people who have been affected by trauma, and when and how to bring the healing of Christ. Let's first consider what is known about the effect that severely damaging life events can have on the mental and emotional makeup of a person.

UNDERSTANDING EXTREME TRAUMA

Let's get some perspective. The morally ugly underbelly of American life is difficult to quantify, and even more difficult to emotionally absorb. But statistically, here is what we do know regarding those damaged souls living among us.[1]

- About three million children a year are victims of reported child abuse; 28 percent of the abuse is physical and 21 percent is sexual. Eighty percent of 21-year-olds who reported abuse suffer from one or more identifiable psychological disorders.

- More than 70 percent of children who die as a result of abuse are two years of age or younger.

- Approximately 10 percent of children in America suffer disability or chronic illness as the result of abuse and neglect.

- Statistics of rape, sexual abuse, and incest reveal that 44 percent of victims are under 18; 68 percent of assaults are never reported to authorities; one out of every six women will experience attempted or completed rape in her lifetime; and 15 percent of sexual abuse victims are under the age of 12. (All victims are six times more likely to suffer from post-traumatic stress disorder, 26 times more likely to abuse drugs, and four times more likely to contemplate suicide.)

- One in five American women have been raped, assaulted, or sexually violated during their lifetime, most of them by their early to mid-20s.

Obviously, these kinds of reportable statistics could fill a book, but my purpose here is to present a quick glimpse at the immensity of the abuse problem in America. Many of these women and men attend your churches and go to your Bible studies. They mostly suffer in silence for fear their inner torment will be exposed. It isn't that they don't want to tell. Rather they fear that if they do break their silence they will be shunned or treated with sympathy without real empathy.

PTSD as a Pathway to Demonization

The most important point I make at the beginning of this chapter is that almost all of the individuals represented by the above statistics suffer from post-traumatic stress disorder (PTSD).

Before the mental health sciences got a grip on this disorder, this is what we used to call "shell shock," speaking of soldiers returning from World War II, Korea, or Viet Nam. Sometimes we just said they had "battle fatigue" and allowed them the courtesy of silence to brood over their misery without asking any penetrating questions. Today, we understand that PTSD can occur outside of wartime trauma; indeed, the battlefield may be one's own home beset with domestic violence, incest, physical abuse, or emotional torment. It's crucial to understand that PTSD is worse when it is the result of repeated trauma, and when trauma is first suffered in early childhood, the time when a person's mind is determining its perspective on how safe one's existence may or may not be. When a small child suffers severe abuse, the message to the infant is clear—the world is a fearful place. Worse yet, PTSD often sets off a cascade of many ancillary health problems such as heart disease, depression, diabetes, and addiction.

Perhaps the worst thing a victim of trauma can do is hide away and suffer in silence. Here's why. The "fight or flight" response to severe trauma can be mitigated by talk therapy or the friendship of a kind listener who helps the suffering individual process pain and put it into perspective. When there has been some kind of healthy emotional outlet for the trauma to be expressed, then something called "fear extinction" takes over; the high level of adrenaline-rushed terror will eventually subside. When there is no one to talk to or no way to escape repeated trauma, PTSD results.

Of course, deliverance ministers recognize the hand of Satan in such situations, keeping people in bondage by encouraging them to build walls of protection to keep out anyone and everything. Sadly, that may include even those kind-hearted individuals who would listen and help or even spiritually intervene. In fact, according to a study at the University of Washington, in cases where people were allowed to vividly recall their terrifying experiences and talk through them, less than half of them went on to develop PTSD as of three months afterward.

Of particular interest to those involved in deliverance is the discovery that about 30 percent of susceptibility to PTSD is genetically inherited. (See the explanation in chapter three regarding the new science of epigenetics.) Researchers have found a direct generational link between the stress of previous ancestors and the susceptibility of the offspring to develop PTSD more severely than they might have otherwise. Clearly, this business of generational curses, explained in explicit detail in my book *Curse Breaking*, is scientifically as well as spiritually supportable.

The Role of Trauma in Demonization

I often tell people who seek my help that they can tell me anything—*anything.* And they do. Often, I'm the first person to whom they've ever bared their soul. The reasons for this are several. They are embarrassed to speak of things that are so highly personal and humiliating. They've never been through a counseling process during which an individual is encouraged to speak about his or her deepest hurts. But most of all, they think that no one will believe them. I understand this reluctance. What has happened to them may be so far outside normal limits, so egregious, so unthinkable, that only the most seasoned therapist or deliverance minister would be aware such abuse exists.

Consider the brief summaries of actual cases I will share in this chapter. Names have been changed and nonessential details have been altered to preserve confidentiality; but none of the horrible facts have been fictionalized. (Furthermore, these are not the worst stories of trauma that I have heard.) So, fasten your spiritual seat belt and step into a world of unimaginably demonic evil and diabolical machinations far more perverse than any human mind could conjure. These accounts are all true, confirmed by intensive investigation and attested to by the interrogated demons who gleefully admit what they had done. My purpose is not to shock but to make readers aware of the immense trauma too many have suffered, which evil spirits have planned and implemented. By revealing extreme evils of this sort, I pray that many more Christians will choose to get involved in healing and deliverance ministries to help end such suffering.

Important note: These case studies are condensed. They are not all-inclusive transcripts of every salient fact related to the deliverance process. I have not included the steps by which demons were confronted and expelled. Neither have I explained the confessional approach to healing. All this, and more, is found in our online study program, the International School of Exorcism. In this chapter of this book, I mainly note the relevant facts of each case so that the reader can grasp the extent of trauma some have experienced.

TRAUMA CASE STUDIES

Case Study #1: Vanessa

> Age 39. Two illegitimate children: son (age 20), a cocaine addict; and daughter (age 17), involved in Wicca. Two failed marriages; currently living with an alcoholic boyfriend.

How does one woman make so many mistakes in life choices? Vanessa was raised by a physically abusive father and an emotionally ill mother. Vanessa first got pregnant and had an abortion at age 16. Both sides of her bloodline abused alcohol. Her maternal grandfather was a serial adulterer. Her paternal grandmother had practiced witchcraft (making baby-sex predictions, conducting the occasional séance, concocting folk healing remedies, etc.). This evil grandmother hated Vanessa from the day she was born. During Personal Encounter sessions with Vanessa, we discovered a dissociated child alter with the memory of being molested by her maternal grandfather.

Much of the generational evil was traced to a 20-generation curse on the father's Irish side, going back to ancient Druid rituals of human sacrifice. This curse was empowered by another bloodline malediction linked to Vanessa's maternal bloodline. This demonic chain went back 17 generations to blood covenants in honor of ancient Nordic deities, including Thor and Odin. The curses were broken, the demons were cast out, and Vanessa eventually severed lustful soul ties with her live-in lover. Her son is in rehab, and her daughter receives ministry from one of our nearby deliverance teams. I have ministered to her in several additional Skype sessions to mop up previously undiscovered demons.

She has enrolled in our International School of Exorcism and is training to help others who, like her, were raised in dysfunctional families. Vanessa is making great progress to understand how she was driven to make such bad life choices. Vanessa is cautiously preparing for the next stage of her life and learning from Christian books and counseling how to find a spiritually healthy mate to bond with.

Case Study #2: Richard

> Age 55. Three children, one daughter and two sons, both addicted to drugs. Three failed marriages. All three children are illegitimate (borne by women Richard didn't marry). He was very smart, but had made extremely unwise life choices. Two unsuccessful suicide attempts.

Like so many people I've helped during Encounter sessions, Richard's problems went back to a neglected childhood and a verbally abusive upbringing. His mother was mentally ill and often told Richard that he was "stupid." His dad looked at pornography constantly, and Richard's mom didn't stop it. Thus, from the age of about nine, Richard became addicted to pornography and drugs, starting with marijuana.

Once the demons were interrogated, I also discovered that, unbeknownst to Richard, his entire life had been hindered by a curse of Perversion and Lust. In fact, I discovered that Richard's great-great-grandfather was a 32nd-degree Mason. In the Lodge, Grandpa had actually made a pact with Satan under the cover of Masonic secrecy. What really made this exorcism unusual was the discovery that a forebear of Richard was Muslim who murdered both Christians and Jews because of a personal jihad mission.

I called forth the Strong Man of this curse. Even though Jezebel, Lust, Murder, and Incest were attacking Richard, it was Perversion who claimed the top dog ranking of evil within. There was so much incest, infidelity, divorces, and hate in his bloodline that Perversion of religion and sexuality stood at the top of this demonic pile-up. And because this demon went back 75 generations, hundreds of years, it required an exorcism tinged with violence to win the battle for Christ. The demon of jihad was not easy to expel, as the reader may assume. But in end, after many hours of healing work to confront Richard's personal pain, the demons had no more legal ground to occupy.

Case Study #3: Abigal

> Mother, aged 42, concerned for her 13-year-old daughter Olivia because she was cutting herself and pulling out her hair. Abigal herself had been sexually molested multiple times. Olivia also heard voices and saw demons; doctors had determined that Olivia had a variety of mental problems.

Before I met with Abigal and her daughter, I had already made a prospective diagnosis. I share this preliminary analysis to give you insights into my thought processes as I prepared for ministry. Whenever possible, it's always good to have a solid "game plan" to know what can be gleaned before a face-to-face meeting. Based on what you've learned so far in this book, note the scenarios that played out in my mind.

1. Nothing in Abigal's request for help said anything about a husband/father. I therefore assumed that Olivia's father was dead or there

had been a marital split. Either way, she likely had no father figure who played a significant role in her life. Otherwise, Abigal would have referred to her husband's involvement and concerns about this ordeal.

2.   I further assumed that Olivia was living in a dysfunctional home, one likely plagued with strife or acrimonious behavior; that she probably felt abandoned, rejected, or both; and that therefore, her self-injurious actions were either a cry for help or an acting out of anger toward her parents, and possibly God.

3.   The hearing of voices might mean that Olivia suffered from dissociated personality states and was therefore unconsciously eavesdropping on internal conversations between her fragmented soul parts. I would need to quickly focus on finding any alter personalities that may have believed the lie that Olivia is worthless. That feeling of unworthiness had likely been reinforced by one or both of her parents. Thus I would be facing a parent problem as much as a teen problem.

4.   Her outbursts of life-threatening behavior lent credence to the possibility that she suffered from demonic influences, especially since the doctors couldn't find a root cause of her actions; they were only trying to mitigate her symptoms with medication.

5.   One of my first tasks would be to find a point of connection with Olivia by asking about her personal life, for example what activities or hobbies held her interest. My guess was that there were none. I would probably find out that she was a loner, constantly recycling her painful past without the benefit of any objective input. After making the personal connection, I would then proceed to evoke any dissociated alters and find out which fragmented parts were on a collision course with death.

6.   I would want to know as much as possible about the family history of both parents. Most cases involving childhood sexual molestation are rooted in generational sexual sin of some kind. I'd try to learn if any family member ever practiced any form of witchcraft or folk magic. Had any ancestors committed murder, belonged to a cult, or indulged in criminal behavior? My working premise would be that Olivia's predicament was fostered by many generations of submission to Satan through evil deeds. I needed to find that link.

7.   If possible, I'd want to engage the parents and assess their spiritual condition in depth to see what doors to the devil they had opened. The family dynamic was obviously traumatized as a whole, and Olivia had gotten the backhand of a curse affecting everyone in the immediate family.

As a postscript, the intervention was successful. Most of my spiritual hunches were right. Dad was out of the scene, though divorce proceedings were not finalized. Olivia suffered the pain of being caught in the middle of parental power plays, and had become a pawn for both parents to manipulate. It turns out that Abigal's ancestors came from a long line of Caribbean pirates and slave-traders. Her soon-to-be ex had ancestors steeped in Freemasonry. Both parents and their forebears had opened multiple doors to demonization. It was an arduous process to bring all the parties to the table for forgiveness and reconciliation. But when that was accomplished, the floodgates of evil were laid open. There was much hugging, crying, and confessing of failures of all kinds, and in the end there was a dramatic deliverance.

The word we received a year after the Personal Encounter session was that Abigal and her husband had called off the divorce and were seeing a marriage counselor. Olivia was being homeschooled in a supportive environment that brought her faith into focus. With her demons cast out, she was free to make more rational decisions. Her major traumas were worked through with the help of a conscientious therapist and a lot of prayer. The story ended well because both Olivia and Abigal had their demons removed and gained an entirely new perspective on life.

Case Study #4: Barbara

Age: mid-50s. Father had beaten her mercilessly in the name of God. Tormenting nightmares. Father was sexually perverted and Barbara was constantly raped at night by evil spirits.

Those who have gone through a series of inexplicable traumas often find it difficult to engage in ordinary situations. Tormented mentally, they may leave the church early in life or cease attending at all. Repeated instances of domestic violence and extremely harsh physical discipline make it hard to receive unconditional acceptance in any form. What made things worse for Barbara was her father's justification for the violent beatings—he portrayed himself as the instrument of God, and the beatings were meant to foster her obedience. At times Barbara had been forced to eat from a dog dish with her hands bound. Her father once made her stand outside on the porch all night in below-freezing temperatures with only her nightgown for clothing. Perhaps even worse, her father owned a bar and had her dance topless for his customers. Still an attractive woman, she had never been married, and she felt obligated to visit her parents in a nursing home every day.

When Barbara's demons were confronted, they responded arrogantly. "We've marked her like a dog," they bragged. These demons tormented her in so many ways. At night they attacked her with perverted nightmares. She often awoke to a sensation that she was being raped. Thinking that she would be diagnosed as schizophrenic and institutionalized, she clung tenaciously to her faith, which was the only spiritual and emotional anchor she had. With that as a starting point, I led Barbara in a simple prayer of breaking curses on her and on behalf of her ancestors. A demon manifested almost instantly, claiming to be chief among all the evil spirits who had set out to destroy her. It took several hours to disengage Barbara from all the emotional pain that she had suffered from her father. When the exorcism had rooted out most, if not all, of her demons, I explained the intricate web of terror in which she had lived since childhood. Her Strong Man was the spirit of Anti-Christ, who entered via the open door of her father. Her father had claimed to be a Christian, but he violated his biblical responsibility to love, nurture, and guide Barbara's life with healthy spiritual leadership. Instead, he had induced trauma in his daughter, which made her an easy target for Satan.

Case Study #5: Allen

Age 43. Twice divorced; high-school math teacher. Spiritually hindered by lust and depression. Mother practiced Santeria and took Allen to rituals. Raped by an older cousin at age eight and raped again by an uncle at age 13. Parents used pornography openly and threw parties with group sex that Allen had to watch.

The reader might well conclude that Allen suffered from sexual identity issues, and he did. In addition to the above, Allen was also molested by his own father. Social Services finally concluded the home was unfit, so Allen spent his teen years living in eight foster homes. In two of them, the sexual abuse continued. He had two older brothers, one institutionalized with schizophrenia and the other in prison for attempted murder. Not surprisingly, Allen had made four suicide attempts and had come to me as a last resort. Needless to say, the fingerprint of Satan was all over Allen's life.

Before I could begin any exorcism procedures, it was necessary to engage in extensive inner healing to deal with the emotional damage from all the sexual abuse. Each violation had been an entry point for demons, and the demonic infrastructure inside Allen was complex and deeply rooted. During our ministry time, which lasted more than six hours, our focus was on bringing the hope and presence of Christ to every area of his life. As we did, the demons fought violently to maintain control. We made a list of all those who had wronged him. We broke all soul-tie connections with the depraved individuals who had violated him. We then instructed Allen to begin the process of extending forgiveness to all who had harmed him. That wasn't easy, and as Allen would try to speak mercy to those who abused him, one demon after another surfaced to interfere. Eventually all the main areas of trauma were healed, all feelings of bitterness were released to the Lord, and we could proceed to exorcise the demons.

TRAUMA SUMMARIES

One intent of this chapter is to provide the reader with as much understanding as possible regarding just how severe the trauma quotient is in American culture. If you are not an experienced therapist, longtime social worker, or seasoned deliverance minister, there is no way to grasp the amount and the intensity of the trauma that is being experienced daily by the people around you. Beneath the surface of society's apparent normalcy is vice and hellishness no human mind could conceive of and no non-traumatized mind could perceive or believe. What is happening behind the scenes to your family, friends, and acquaintances is fiendish, and it hides behind walls of evils of which none dare speak.

From my actual case files here are a few of the pleas for help that reach my office every day. Most pastors never hear of such outrages, because these desperate people would never ask help from the cool, hip pastor who's more concerned about his latest tattoo or trendy video composite that passes for a sermon. These hurting hearts cry out from behind their walls of shame to be validated, but they can't find help in today's market-based worship centers with their spectacular light shows and dumbed-down litanies of shallow slogans.

You may not like what you are about to read, which will offend your sensibilities (as well it should). It may interfere somewhat with your sleep tonight, and I pray that in some cases it does, because I want people to stake a claim to genuine discipleship by being introduced to the bleeding heart of America. I have only edited these pleas for confidentiality and, in some cases, brevity. And these are just a handful of cases, taken from thousands, in order to show you the real, raw truth about the lost and floundering souls around you.

Shelly: Please help. I'm 49. I was the result of my mom's one-night stand. Never knew my dad. I was molested by both males and females at a young age. Raped repeatedly. Pregnant at 15. Attempted suicide many times starting at 13. Too many abortions to remember. My doctor says I am PTSD. I became a Christian but struggle with rejection and socializing. I just want to be free.

Connor: I am 42 and the oldest in our family. I have two siblings. We live in hell and suffering. My father beat and threatened my mother. As a small child I watched him put a loaded gun to her head. He finally left and Mom raised us alone. None of us are married. We're all filled with anger, hoarding, stealing, and alcoholism. We always have accidents and live in depression. Please bring us hope before it's too late. Stop this for the sake of future generations. I beg you.

Connie: I am battling demons. Televisions turn off and on by themselves. Doors slam and no one entered or left the room. Food disappears from my fridge. I leave things in one place and they turn up in another. Animals that come on my property wail and screech. Lights flicker on and off. An electrician couldn't find what is happening. Sometimes there is a foul stench in the house. I should probably tell you that I played with the Ouija board a lot as a kid and my dad's sister was really strange. She said she came from a long line of gypsies. No one, not even my own pastor, believes me, and I'm slowing losing my mind. I am so desperate.

Ruby: I need an exorcism! I was previously involved in Satanism and spells. Now I am literally held captive in my home. If I even say the word "God" they physically attack me. Throw me around and sexually assault me. I resorted to being a mean Satanist again just to save my life. I feel scared, sad, and let down. I pray to God and confess my sins. I ask for protection, but nothing gets better. Please, please help.

Rita: The demonic attacks started when my husband and I got married. We've both been sick for a month at a time. Both of us have horrible nightmares of killing, war, bloody things. We hear the demons walk into our bedroom at night. They paralyze both of us. One night my husband spoke in a female voice. Then strange sounds came out of his mouth. We are filled with the Holy Ghost so how can this happen? Please help us. We can't tell anyone, as they would think we are crazy.

Chase: Out of nowhere I get sudden chills. My pets can sense whatever it is. It is like I am living in my own horror movie. If I sing or play Christian songs the lights go off. I see this very vivid, pale creature being locked in my room, even when the door is not locked. A child's voice cries out "Mommy, Mommy." I have an old music box that starts up by itself. I am a baptized Christian and don't understand how this can happen.

Nolan: A few years ago I joined a church that believed everyone needed demons cast out. I didn't think I had demons, but went along and pretended to manifest. It was so traumatizing. Actually, I opened a door to demons by pretending to be possessed, and now I am tormented. Now I hear voices telling me to commit the most perverse acts, even on babies. I lie about my problems because no one would ever believe my story. When I try to sleep hideous beings appear to me and tell me to join them or I'll always suffer like this. I don't know anyone but you who can help me.

Emily: I am a highly paid person in a very professional field, and I'm a Christian. But if I don't fix some things, I know it will all crash. My parents were both alcoholics and swingers. I remember them taking me to orgy parties when I was only five. I was conceived illegitimately, and I'm not even sure that my "dad" is my real dad. I started masturbating at that age because of what I saw. There was a lot of domestic violence. I saw my dad put a shotgun to mom's head and threaten to pull the trigger. My maternal grandfather molested me. So did a brother. I can't even wear underwear without being sexually aroused. I'll do whatever I need to see you and get spiritual help.

Cecile: I am from several Caribbean islands. All the men on my dad's side were Freemasons. I've heard that when I was young, my father sold my soul in a Mason ceremony to clear a debt. On my mother's side there was a lot of witchcraft. I was sick at age four and my mum took me to a healer woman who bathed me in sea water and cut my arm in several places to mix blood with the water. I was terrified. Since then I've suffered all kinds of sicknesses, none of which the doctors can find a cure for. Can you help me?

Blake: My story may seem a bit unreal, but it's all true. As a kid, my dad constantly cheated on my mom, and even took me on his dates with other women. Dad once took a kitchen knife and threatened to stab both me and my mom. He threw the knife at her and missed by inches. Mom finally dumped him after all the cheating, alcohol, and gambling. She went through more marriages before I left home, each one worse than before. My brother became a heroin addict and a Satanist to get away from things. He's in prison now. At six I was molested by a babysitter. I have come to admit that my own mother incested me when I was still quite young. Let's say we took some strange baths together. I am ashamed to say I have thoughts of molesting other children and even killing them. Is there any hope for a person like me? I can't tell this to anyone.

RESPONDING TO TRAUMA CASE STUDIES AND SUMMARIES

To those with limited practical experience in the ministry of deliverance, and particularly those who have not completed the course studies of our International School of Exorcism, these accounts may seem overwhelming. If someone such as this approached you, either with a formal request for help or an informal expression of angst, what should you do? Unfortunately, too many Christians might feel uncomfortable and send such a person away with the dismissive equivalent of James's tongue-in-check rebuke, "Depart in peace, be warmed and filled" (James 2:16). James declared that it is a moral crime to send away those who are "destitute" without offering to them "the things which are needed for the body." This, James says, is faith without works, which is lifeless, "dead" (James 2:16). The individuals described above have been emotionally deprived; through severe trauma, they were denied life's necessities of the soul. We dare not send them away without at least attempting to meet their needs.

"But where," some might ask, "do I start?" Passing hurting individuals off with the phone number of a pastor or Christian counselor may not be the most helpful thing to do at such a crucial moment, because when someone starts speaking openly about trauma, it seldom happens without an agonizing process of gradually opening up. Their revelation of personal pain may be the crack in their façade of self-protection that's needed to offer them true hope in Christ. If the Holy Spirit seems to be leading to a discussion of painful wounds, don't be intimidated. Remember what you've learned in this book and put it into action. Remember, you are looking for the fingerprint of Satan. This is your chance to crack the code of evil and begin bringing down Satan's kingdom of trauma so the healing of Christ can be received.

The reader has been instructed early in the book to embark on a methodical decipherment of what the devil has done. Start with those "Ten Things You Need to Know" noted in chapter two, including age, occupation, education, etc. Quickly and briefly ask well-placed questions to identify the basic demonic openings in the family structure, as I instructed in chapter three. Then, taking a cue from chapter four, begin analyzing the individual's belief system. Ask a few well-placed questions to see if there is anything openly demonic in the person's life (chapter five), and then see what mental and physical issues (chapter six) may be at the root of his or her personal torment. Finally, probe deeper into the person's emotional world (chapter seven) to discern what unhealthy areas of perception have dominated his or her thinking.

Perhaps this all sounds complicated, but the more often this process is engaged, the easier it will become. The serious student of healing and deliverance will gradually become more and more comfortable with this paradigm and learn when to trust the Holy Spirit to stop at any particular point to pray or actually confront an evil spirit. I have given this approach to ministry in its totality, but wisdom and the cultivation of spiritual gifts will heighten your sensitivity as to when you have gone far enough and when you need to stop for immediate, prayerful intervention.

PERSPECTIVE

How does reading these accounts of trauma affect you? Do you wish you hadn't heard them? Do you somewhere in the back of your mind think that these people are just losers and will complain no matter what happens? Are you upset with how bluntly they explain their lives? Would your solution be to send them a gospel tract and tell them that Jesus is their hope if they'll just trust in Him? Needless to say, all these responses are inadequate.

Please face the fact that far too may responses to this level of need are dismissive. Too many American believers are narcissistically focused on their own walk of faith, their personal path to prosperity, self-satisfying "signs and wonders," or their pet theological fads. Don't mistake me. I believe in a supernatural God who does amazing things that constantly confound our human wisdom. But we cannot allow spiritual eccentricities to turn us away from the profound pain being suffered by so many, pain that only the properly trained deliverance minister will be able to sort out, with God's help.

This book may not have all the answers you need to faithfully and effectively reach those in spiritual bondage. But I pray that it contains a lot more information than you ever imagined would be helpful in the deliverance process. The command of Christ to cast out demons is clear, so let's get on with the job before us: freeing those enslaved to Satan.

In the Synoptic Gospels of Matthew, Mark, and Luke there are five anecdotal accounts of Christ casting out demons with specific individuals. They are:

1.   Two demon-possessed men who were delivered in the country of the Gergesenes; the demon calling itself "Legion" (Matthew 8, Mark 5, and Luke 8).

2.   The Canaanite woman with a demon-possessed daughter (Matthew 5 and Mark 7).

3. The father whose son would fall into fire and water (Matthew 17, Mark 9, and Luke 9).

4. The man with an unclean spirit in the synagogue (Mark 1 and Luke 4).

5. The daughter of Abraham with a spirit of infirmity (Luke 13).

Entire sermons could be preached, even whole books written, about any one of these instances. Consider what may be learned from these accounts:

1. Demonization is associated with violence, nudity, and self-injury (Legion).

2. Faith is necessary for deliverance (Canaanite woman).

3. Demons can hide in a religious environment (man in synagogue).

4. Demons are inherited (man in synagogue, Canaanite woman, man with self-destructive son).

5. Demons try to kill their victims (man with son, Legion).

6. Christians can have demons (daughter of Abraham, man in synagogue).

7. Jesus allowed demons to speak (Legion, man in synagogue).

8. Jesus interrogated demons (Legion).

9.   Parental authority can deliver a child (Canaanite woman).

10.   Some exorcisms take time/fasting/prayer (man with self-destructive son).

11.   Demons may manifest violently (man with self-destructive son, Legion, man in synagogue).

12.   Demons cause disease as well as spiritual torment (daughter of Abraham).

I end with this note to demonstrate how little we really understand about the kingdom of evil and all its operations. The reader might well be shaken by what is above that shatters commonly held assumptions regarding demonic activity. Get the point? In the Christian community at large, there is far too much arrogance about what some Christian leaders think they know regarding spiritual warfare but which they have little researched and even less experienced. Let us all humble ourselves before the Lord of Glory and do all that we can to fulfill the clear command of Christ that the signs of His power and authority will be revealed: "In My name they will cast out demons" (Mark 16:17).

NOTE

1.   This information is from sources such as Childhelp and the National Child Abuse Hotline; American Humane Association; Rape, Abuse, and Incest National Network; Rape Crisis Center; and International Report, "The Economist," October 24, 2015.

About Bob Larson

Rev. Bob Larson is the world's foremost expert on supernatural phenomena. He has ministered in over 100 countries and has appeared on shows such as *Oprah, The O'Reilly Factor, Good Morning America, Nightline, CNN News,* and *Dr. Phil.* Numerous networks have produced documentaries about Bob, and he has also been featured in major newspapers. He is the author of 35 books, which have been translated into more than a dozen languages, and is the founder of the online International School of Exorcism®.